Global Strategy

Douglas Lamont

- ■ Fast track route to mastering all aspects of global strategy

- ■ Covers all the fundamentals of successful global strategy, from market entry tactics to understanding local regulations, and from understanding country risk to finding sales and marketing opportunities

- ■ Examples and lessons from some of the world's most successful businesses, including Wal-Mart, Tesco and MSN, and ideas from the smartest strategy gurus

- ■ Includes a glossary of key concepts and a comprehensive resources guide

>> EXPRESS EXEC.COM <<
essential management thinking at your fingertips

First published 2002 by
Capstone Publishing (a Wiley company)
8 Newtec Place
Magdalen Road
Oxford OX4 1RE
United Kingdom
http://www.capstoneideas.com

CIP catalogue records for this book are available from the British Library and the US Library of Congress

ISBN 978-1-84112-190-1

This book is printed on acid-free paper

Substantial discounts on bulk quantities of Capstone books are available to corporations, professional associations and other organizations. Please contact Capstone for more details on +44 (0)1865 798 623 or (fax) +44 (0)1865 240 941 or (e-mail) info@wiley-capstone.co.uk

Contents

Introduction to ExpressExec

ExpressExec is 3 million words of the latest management thinking compiled into 10 modules. Each module contains 10 individual titles forming a comprehensive resource of current business practice written by leading practitioners in their field. From brand management to balanced scorecard, ExpressExec enables you to grasp the key concepts behind each subject and implement the theory immediately. Each of the 100 titles is available in print and electronic formats.

Through the ExpressExec.com Website you will discover that you can access the complete resource in a number of ways:

» printed books or e-books;
» e-content – PDF or XML (for licensed syndication) adding value to an intranet or Internet site;
» a corporate e-learning/knowledge management solution providing a cost-effective platform for developing skills and sharing knowledge within an organization;
» bespoke delivery – tailored solutions to solve your need.

Why not visit www.expressexec.com and register for free key management briefings, a monthly newsletter and interactive skills checklists. Share your ideas about ExpressExec and your thoughts about business today.

Please contact elound@wiley-capstone.co.uk for more information.

Introduction

Why global strategy is important and why it will be even more important in the global and electronic economy.

Why is global strategy important today? Why will it be important tomorrow? Here are six reasons why global strategy is crucial to the world's prosperity:

» It gives attention to the effect of free trade area (FTA) rules and national laws on the strategic management decision of firms.
» It reduces the impact of country risk (that is, national barriers to trade and investment) on international decision making by multinational firms.
» It shows why foreign direct investments, acquisitions, equity joint ventures, non-equity partnerships and alliances, licensing, and franchising work well under different national norms of intrusion into the local economy.
» It gives consumers the opportunity for improved standards of living, enhanced lifestyles, and a wider choice of goods and services.
» It offers world-class, standardized products, but uses locally produced goods when national culture requires a modification in the product mix.
» It provides a venue for global brands to be sold worldwide, regional brands to be sold within the free trade area, and national brands to be sold locally.

GLOBAL STRATEGY

International executives make the following business decisions about global strategy, whether these are for all markets worldwide, within the home and neighboring country markets of free trade agreements (FTAs), or for national markets alone. These go under the rubric of the product life cycle:

» **Entry**: Be first, or go in second or later. Also known as first-mover advantage.
» **Invest**: Build new buildings and buy new equipment. Also known as ''greenfield'' investments.
» **Expand**: Take over foreign subsidiaries, undertake equity joint ventures, form partnerships and strategic alliances, do licensing and franchising deals. Also known as foreign direct investments.

» **Deepen**: Manufacture goods and services to gain scale economies, and distribute these products to gain scope economies. Also known as product assembly, subcontracting, outsourcing, technology, new product development, channels of distribution.

» **Build out**: Dominate home market, go into neighboring country markets and, eventually, into most of the world's markets. Also known as local, regional, and global brand management.

» **Terminate**: Reduce the number of investments, sell joint ventures to partners, and cancel alliances. Also known as failure in terms of growth in sales, returns on investment, and a slowdown in cash flow.

Global strategy combines ideas about free trade, competition, and management with lessons learned from practical business experience. In this book, we focus on the firm's ability to obtain substantial competitive advantage through a set of global and global-regional strategies.

GLOBAL-REGIONAL STRATEGY

Some international business executives think in terms of a comprehensive effort to manufacture and sell products worldwide, and label this their global strategy. Other international managers think in terms of regional (that is, North American Free Trade Agreement (NAFTA)) and local (e.g., the United States, Canada, or Mexico) approaches towards manufacturing and marketing, but they too label this their global strategy. Regretfully, the term global strategy means two different things among international executives, managers, and marketers.

The few truly global firms, such as Nestlé and Philips, pursue a global strategy in all world markets. The larger number of multinational firms, such as Royal Dutch Shell, Unilever, McDonald's, Procter & Gamble, Interbrew, and Sony, pursue both a global strategy in some world markets and a regional strategy in other world markets (for example, in the European Union, the North American Free Trade Area, and in Japan). The vast number of multi-domestic firms, such as Wal-Mart, Carrefour, Ikea, and other retail chains, pursue both regional and local international marketing strategies.

This great divide in management's perception about global strategy comes from cultural differences between common markets and free trade agreements, among developed and emerging nation-states, and by global, multinational, and multi-domestic firms and their national business management.

Let's try to sort these out and make some sense to these two different approaches towards global strategy.

Pro-global strategy

Professor Paul Simmonds of Florida State University in Tallahassee, Florida, USA says that business firms are the true generators of economic activity. They work and prosper within a global business environment of market interdependency or linkages of standardized products and services. These firms leverage their resources to compete worldwide with franchising, global branding, and global product, promotion, and pricing strategies. Their world is the global diffusion of knowledge in which they take advantage of opportunities wherever they may be.

Pro-regional strategy

Professor Alan Rugman of Indiana University in Bloomington, Indiana, USA says that countries (and their supra-national FTAs) are the true generators of economic activity. Sovereign nation-states reduce the national barriers to trade, especially with their neighbors and partners in the FTAs. Since nations are more important than firms, globalization is a myth. Instead, international trade and investment takes place within the North American Free Trade Area, the European Union, and Japan's trade and investment links with South East Asia and China. Successful firms do business in all three regions, but they tend to dominate only one of these regions.

Common language

Let's agree with Simmonds that global, multinational, multi-local, and domestic firms are the true generators of economic activity. They make crucial decisions about foreign direct investments, rollout of foreign-sourced products and services in overseas markets, and repatriation of profits. Let's agree with Rugman that nation-states individually or through FTAs set the boundaries for trade and investment within regional economies and the global economy at large. Therefore, global strategy depends on proactive choices of both business firms and nation-states. Their joint work means success or failure in international business.

KEY LESSONS

Douglas Lamont, the author of nine books on international investments, international business, international marketing, and global strategy, takes this point of view. In his global marketing book for this series, he shows how McDonald's, the king of fast-food dining, pursues a global brand marketing strategy in all possible markets worldwide. In this book on global strategy, he offers Wal-Mart, the king of discount retailing, as an example of the dominant firm within a regional FTA, or NAFTA, and as an also-ran in selected European Union (EU) and Mercosur or southern South American markets.

Both McDonald's and Wal-Mart are American-owned firms that dominate their home US market; to stay ahead of their competition they had to diversify internationally. McDonald's chose a pure global strategy without worrying a great deal about the pros and cons of country risk. On the other hand, Wal-Mart selected a global-regional strategy, and it has made some mistakes in judging the importance of economic, cultural, and business risks within local countries. Let's look at the lessons from the Wal-Mart case (Readers are directed to the global marketing book in this series for the lessons from the McDonald's case.):

1 Wal-Mart offers multinationals and multi-local firms a road map for building up a set of regional subsidiaries within a free trade area. Dominate the home market of the US and the neighboring country markets to the north and south.
2 Wal-Mart represents the world's discount retail culture. Create the image of a regional American firm that fits in well in Canada and Mexico, and fix its image as an American firm that does not fit in well with cultures in distance lands, such as Germany and Argentina.
3 Wal-Mart trains local people as managers, employees, and information specialists. Build up loyalty to the firm.

4 Wal-Mart offers improvements in its use of information technology as it seeks better and faster ways to buy and sell merchandise. Show innovation in merchandising, stocking shelves, pricing, and logistics.

CASE: WAL-MART

Wal-Mart, a discount retailer, dominates its home market, the USA. It has a high-profile brand image for innovative merchandising, rapid turnover of goods, and low prices. Its suppliers deliver clothes on hangers and put bicycles and other equipment together with the retail prices already marked on the products; these suppliers also put the canned and boxed goods on the shelves of the chain store, and lock the computers and TVs to them. Wal-Mart has built up strong customer loyalty from its home base in Bentonville, Arkansas, in rural USA.

Country risk: Canada

Canada's population is 31 million with about 19 million English-speaking Canadians (or Anglophones) and 12 million French-speaking Canadians (or Francophones). The USA is nine times larger in population. Canada's national economy is equivalent to the size of the state of California's economy. Although Canada is one of the G7 or major industrialized countries, its GDP per capita is lower than the US $33,000 in the USA. Also, Canadian wages in manufacturing are lower and some of its "best and brightest" people migrate to the USA. Moreover, the foreign exchange value of the Canadian dollar is almost 40 percent lower than the US dollar. Hence, Canadians feel poorer economically when they compare themselves to Americans.

On the other hand, Canadians feel richer than their neighbors in the USA in terms of specific values and lifestyles. They practice a wait-and-see, more conservative attitude towards new things and ideas. Canadians believe their national health service is more equitable to all Canadians. And they think of their federal and provincial governments as generally free of the rampant lobbying found in Washington, DC. Canadians think of themselves as more open and willing to accept foreign immigrants from all over the world.

In terms of strategy and marketing, English-speaking Canadians and Americans tend to have similar values, lifestyles, attitudes, habits, and customs (or self-reference criteria) about consumption, the quality of goods, the mix of products, packaging, and the acceptance of or rejection of global and regional brands. Hence, McDonald's and other American-owned fast-food establishments compete with Tim Horton's, once Canadian and now owned by Wendy's. Hence, Wal-Mart has become the biggest retailer in Canada, driving out of business such old-line Canadian retailers as T. Eaton's & Company.

Wal-Mart Canada

When Wal-Mart took over 122 down-at-the-heel Woolco stores in Canada from Woolworth's, the US parent, in 1994, Canadians thought that this might be one American cultural invasion too many. Canada already had McDonald's, Pizza Hut, Dunkin Donuts, PBS, CNN, *The Wall Street Journal*, *Time*, Hollywood, NFL, NBA, MLB, GM, Ford, Chrysler, and many other US-owned brands and firms. Even though Canadians had voted themselves into free trade with the USA once in 1989 (the US – Canada FTA) and again in 1994 (NAFTA), Canadians in the mid-1990s had a real apprehension of becoming the 51st state in the American Union, because English-speaking Canadians did not think they could continue to differentiate themselves clearly from Americans. French-speaking Canadians did not have the same apprehension about the USA and its culture because they spoke a different language and were culturally closer to France than the UK. English-speaking Canadians wondered whether Canada's more conservative outlook towards commerce and business would disappear altogether. This has not happened, but Canada is not as free as it once was from litigation over competition policy.

Canadian retail firms in the 1990s wondered rightly whether they would go under with wave after wave of new stores from Sears, Wal-Mart, and others. In fact, T. Eaton's first sold itself to Simpson-Sears and then closed down completely under the onslaught of Wal-Mart and other US-owned retail chains. Other Canadian-owned retail chains bought their competitors out, consolidated the industry, and tried to get ready to compete against the new Canadian-based American retail chains. Most local firms found they could not get their prices down far enough to induce Canadians back into their shops. They had lost the fight, as American Mom & Pop stores and local retail establishments did in the USA during the 1950s and 1960s.

Discount retail culture

Wal-Mart represents the discount retail culture prevalent in the USA and eagerly adopted in Canada. Wal-Mart Canada pushes the same innovations in merchandising, logistics, and information technology as the parent firm did in the USA. Also, Wal-Mart Canada builds up loyalty among employees, managers, and customers. Finally Wal-Mart Canada delivers low prices on its private-label offerings (for example, Sam's Choice and No Boundaries cosmetics).

Notwithstanding these corporate cultural similarities between Wal-Mart's operations in Canada and the USA, Wal-Mart did a careful analysis of the real cultural differences between the two countries. Canadians want to see locally produced Canadian goods in their Wal-Mart stores. The firm obliged and put Canadian-origin canoes, camping equipment, clothes for the outdoors, and fishing rods and lures in their local stores. Also, Canadians want to buy furniture, consumer electronics, and pet supplies at discount chain retailers even though these are not common products in US Wal-Mart stores. Again the firm obliged. Moreover, Wal-Mart puts more inserts into newspapers because this is how Canadians prefer to get their retail advertising. Finally, Wal-Mart helps local Canadian-owned firms (such as Krave's Canada of Winnipeg, Manitoba) gain scale economies and ship to both Canadian and US Wal-Mart stores.

Between the USA and Canada, the discount retail culture is alive and thriving, helped no doubt by the free flow of tariff-free goods across the border between these two NAFTA countries. The same is true in Mexico, but with a several major differences.

Country risk Mexico

Mexico's population is 97 million, with about 90 million who speak Spanish and the rest in the south of Mexico who speak one of the native Indian languages. Among the president and his cabinet, the high-income groups, and the cultural elite that commute to and from New York, Hollywood, and Disneyworld, English is their second language.

Mexico is more than three times the size of Canada in population, but Mexico's national economy is equivalent to the size of the city of Los Angeles, California, USA. Mexico's GDP per capita is about US $5,800 or one-sixth of what it is in Canada. Also, Mexican wages in manufacturing are one-seventh of those in the USA and many of its poor and talented people migrate to the USA. Moreover, the foreign exchange value of the Mexican peso collapses periodically whenever Mexico imports more than it can pay for, or its inflation surges, or its national politics unravel once again. Hence, Mexicans know they are poorer economically when they compare themselves to Americans and Canadians.

On the other hand, Mexicans feel richer than their neighbors in the USA and Canada in terms of specific values and lifestyles. Mexicans are people of the night, and late dinners and social events are more important than working 24 hours, seven days per week. Mexicans take to new things right away, especially if they come from the USA, fit into Mexican values and lifestyles, and offer Mexicans the opportunity to pretend they are really Americans or at least North Americans. Mexicans know their national infrastructure and government are not up to the demands of a modern, NAFTA-induced market economy. They hope that their new president, the anti-ruling party candidate, Vincente Fox, can make things a whole lot better for them over his six-year term.

In terms of strategy and marketing, Mexicans tend to have both similar and dissimilar values, lifestyles, attitudes, habits, and customs (or self-reference criteria) about consumption, the quality of goods, the mix of products, packaging, and the acceptance of or rejection of global and regional brands. Hence, McDonald's and other American-owned fast-food establishments compete with Sanborn's, a Mexican-owned restaurant. Hence, Wal-Mart has become the biggest retailer in Mexico, forcing Palacio de Hierro and Liverpool, both locally owned, to adopt more American retail practices, and driving out of business such old-line American retailers as Sears.

Wal-Mart Mexico

Before Wal-Mart arrived in Mexico, Mexicans would drive from Mexico City, cross the border at Laredo, and shop at Wal-Mart on the American side. Then they would cross the border, pay off their police, and smuggle the goods back to Mexico City. After Wal-Mart went into Mexico as an equity joint venture partner with Cifra, and especially after tariffs were eliminated under NAFTA, Wal-Mart bought US-made goods, shipped truckloads of them to Mexico, and sold them at cheaper prices than could be obtained from other Mexican retail stores, e.g., ConAgra's Act II popcorn. Wal-Mart did the same for Japanese goods made at the northern border plants near the USA, e.g., Sony's Wega line of flat-screen televisions. "It's like shopping in the US!" say Mexicans. They can pretend to be Americans while shopping in the Wal-Mart stores in Mexico City and elsewhere in Mexico. Today, Wal-Mart owns all the stores and has bought out its Mexican joint venture partner.

Wal-Mart in the USA, Canada, and Mexico is a good example of a regional brand for discount retail service. Wal-Mart in North America offers a roadmap for other US companies that seek dominance in their home market and in neighboring countries' markets as well. Wal-Mart has prospered under the tariff-free regime of NAFTA. Others are prospering, too, such as Molson (beer) and Macmillan Bloedel (forest products and packaging) from Canada, and Cemex (cement) and Bimbo (bread and pastries) from Mexico.

Wal-Mart's global-regional strategy

Wal-Mart's success in North America is due in part to the USA dominating NAFTA and its two partners having mostly similar tastes and values in goods and services. Wal-Mart USA could spread its business logic, marketing expertise, and information technology to Canada and Mexico without too many changes in the way it did business in the USA. When Wal-Mart tried this formula in Germany, it failed because its meat selection was made up of different cuts than the Germans were used to, and its prices were higher than those of its competitors. In Argentina, Wal-Mart failed because its jewelry was flashy, colorful, and American, and Argentine women prefer modest, conservative colors, and European-type bracelets, necklaces, and rings. Since 1999, Wal-Mart has tried to become more savvy in its European and Latin American operations, but it has a long way to go to be as successful as it is in North America.

Let's conclude the case by noting that Wal-Mart's NAFTA regional strategy worked. Sales grew very fast. Profits were made quickly. And cash flow could be used to acquire retail chains elsewhere in the world. Let's conclude also that Wal-Mart is not yet a global multinational firm such as McDonald's. North American-style discount retailing may not travel well outside of North America. Time will tell whether Wal-Mart builds out or terminates its investment in Europe and Latin America.

FTA strategy

Wal-Mart's strategic response to the free trade opportunities and constraints placed on its actions by NAFTA include sovereign decisions on tariffs and non-tariff barriers, bi-national decision-making tribunals, cabotage rules for trucking goods across national boundaries, and similarities between Canadians and Americans, and differences between Mexicans and the others. Firms, such as Wal-Mart, design a global-regional strategy to manufacture, ship, and market goods to Canada, the USA, and Mexico. Timing plays a crucial role in the strategic interaction between FTAs and firms. For example, Wal-Mart got into Mexico in the early 1990s and into Canada in 1994, and showed the way for success in North America before US, Canadian, and Mexican regulators had time to formulate their own, perhaps more restrictive, rules and regulations.

Here is a testable hypothesis: Wal-Mart might have done better in terms of sales, profits, and cash flow without the presence of NAFTA. The case discussed above belies this statement. Thus let's draw the following conclusions:

» Wal-Mart carried out complex competitive strategies prior to and after the adoption of NAFTA that led to its success in Canada, the USA, and Mexico.
» Wal-Mart's NAFTA strategy made it possible for the firm's managers to respond to changes in supra-national FTA rules, national legislation in three countries, and social and cultural values and lifestyles among Americans, Canadians, and Mexicans.
» Wal-Mart gives attention to the need for neighboring countries to enter into FTAs and provide a stable frontier for trade and investment analysis by international executives.

SOURCES

Miriam Jordan, "Wal-Mart grows aggressive about Brazil," *The Wall Street Journal*, May 25, 2001, pp. A8, A12.

Douglas Lamont, *Global Marketing* (Oxford, UK: Executive Express, Capstone-Wiley, 2001), Chapter 1.

Dale Luhnow, "How NAFTA helped Wal-Mart transform the Mexican market," *The Wall Street Journal*, August 31, 2001, pp. A1–A2.

Alan M. Rugman, "The myth of global strategy," and Paul Simmonds, "Globalization: another viewpoint," in AIB Newsletter, Second Quarter 2001, pages 11–16.

Bernard Simon, "Canada warms to Wal-Mart," *The New York Times*, September 1, 2001, pp. B1, B3.

Definition of Terms

» What is global strategy and how is it different from management, organizational, market, and public strategies?
» How do corporate views on and government attitudes towards sovereign risk and free trade put a few nation-states on the "hot" countries list for sales and marketing opportunities?

What is global strategy? What terms, interpretations, observations, and frameworks in use today describe global strategy? Which authors give the most important key lessons and case analyses for global strategy? Here are four action items for global strategy:

» **Management strategy**: When management makes trade and investment decisions, it uses a backward induction process. First, define the set of constraints on strategic actions (for example, FTA rules and national regulations). Second, define the set of strategic actions (that is, dominate the home market, go into neighboring country markets, seek sales and marketing opportunities all over the world). And third, define a set of objectives (in terms of growth in sales, increases in market share, and higher returns on investments).

» **Organizational strategy**: When management makes international manufacturing decisions, it determines the boundaries or limits placed on its tasks, choices, and decisions. For example, NAFTA's rules on country of origin force non-North American investors in Mexico to build sufficient plant capacity to add 50 percent value in terms of labor and manufacturing costs, and to utilize enough machinery to change the physical character of the goods moving from Germany, to Mexico, and to the USA. Management can set up its own factory in Mexico, outsource the work to third-party border plants (*maquiladoras*), or hire contract manufacturers (such as Flextronics) to conform to NAFTA's rules on changing the country of origin.

» **Market strategy**: When management makes international marketing decisions, it determines what takes place within and what takes place outside the firm. Questions: Where are product, pricing, promotion, and channel decisions made? Who makes these decisions: the firm, its suppliers, its competitors, or by other firms? When are these decisions delegated to outsiders? In the Wal-Mart example (see Chapter 1), the firm insists its suppliers put clothes on hangers, pre-price them, and roll them out into the aisles of stores in Canada, the USA, and Mexico.

» **Public strategy**: When management makes global strategy decisions, it determines the legal restraints on wholly owned subsidiaries versus equity joint ventures, and the social restraints on the quality, type, and price of merchandise sold in national markets. Before

NAFTA, Wal-Mart took on a Mexican partner to go into Mexico. After the start of NAFTA, Wal-Mart bought out its Mexican partner, and began putting merchandise in its Mexican and Canadian stores that was demanded by local people. For reasons little understood, Wal-Mart failed to do this second step in Germany and Argentina until its management faced a decision to terminate the foreign direct investments altogether.

In the broad fields on international investments, international business, international marketing, and global strategy, executives must choose efficient and effective organizational designs, successful competitive strategies, and management and marketing actions that recognize the public policies of nation-states and their supra-national FTAs.

KEY LESSONS

1 Global management strategy is a process of backward induction in which international executives find out the legal and political boundaries set for them by nation-states and their supra-national FTAs. Provide the minimum number of cabin personnel that are required by the government of the United Kingdom and by the European Union. Offer the British and Irish no-frills air flights, that is, no food, no drinks, no boarding passes, etc., at cheap prices. Make money by carrying out only the essential value chain activities within Go, Ryanair and EasyJet, and paying for all others in the market. Global management strategy that European firms must be on the lookout for innovations from US firms and, of course, vice versa.

2 Global organization strategy links suppliers, contract manufacturers, parts producers, and assemblers via data and information networks. Both NAFTA and the EU endorse sharing manufacturing skills, and the EU permits the accumulation of value (for country of origin purposes) among firms located within Europe. Since free trade does not exist between NAFTA and the EU, both FTAs have their own tariff regimes that put at a disadvantage parts produced in Mexico and the USA and sold in the European Union, and goods manufactured in the UK,

Germany, and Italy and sold in North America. Make money by distributing manufacturing among suppliers, contract manufacturers, parts producers, and assemblers within the value chains of Arm, Aiztron, Prolion, Fresenius, and JCB. Global organization strategy means that European firms must be on the lookout for low-cost opportunities that will keep them competitive against US, Japanese, Chinese, and other firms.

3 Global market strategy asks retail marketing institutions and their customers to determine whether bricks-and-mortar or online retailing or both are appropriate for buying food, clothes, household appliances, and other items. Two years after the debacle of the dotcom revolution, both retailers and customers have decided that bricks-and-mortar retailing is still best for selecting among assortments of goods, and for fulfillment and delivery of purchases; they both believe that online retailing is best for searching for the best price. Of course, catalog shopping has transformed itself into online shopping for some. However, for most people online retailing is still not within their routine social practices because they prefer to go shopping at stores. Retail chains in both NAFTA and the EU have the same set of issues facing them. Wal-Mart's bricks-and-mortar and online operations are a success in Canada and Mexico, and a failure in Germany and Argentina. Tesco's bricks-and-mortar and online operations are a success in the UK and still open to judgment in the USA. Other retail chains, such as Ahold and Carrefour from Europe, are all trying out both traditional and online channels of distribution.

4 Global public strategy requires media firms to pay attention to the Directives from the EU. Brussels seeks to manage competition in the media and telecommunications industries. However, software seems to be excluded from this review. Hence, MSN Europe may find itself in an enviable position against its main rival, AOL Europe.

"HOT" COUNTRIES LIST

Through a backward induction process, outsiders weigh the sovereign risk of government bonds, the foreign exchange value of the national currency, the investment climate for sales and returns on investments, and the brand viability of nation-states. From all of this information, some countries are considered good investments, others are deemed modest opportunities, and still others are thrust into the great pile of bad choices. International executives have a choice, perhaps imperfect, on how to spend their firm's investment dollars. Here is my list of "hot" countries.

Look for sales and marketing opportunities

1 The three NAFTA countries: Mexico for small cars and auto parts; Canada for supplying furniture, computer electronics, and pet supplies to Wal-Mart Canada ; and the USA for new taste sensations in chocolates, hard candy, etc. from products currently popular north and south of the border.

2 The northern European Union countries: Finland and Sweden for wireless telecommunications; and the UK, Germany, and France for traditional industrial goods.

3 The southern EU countries: Spain, Portugal, Italy, and Greece for older technologies that can be adapted for new local uses.

4 The North Asian countries: Japan for the latest in consumer electronics gadgets and Korea for copycat auto and electronics technologies that are cheaper than those from Japan.

5 Mainland China (including Hong Kong and Taiwan) for wireless mobile phones.

6 South East Asia for standardized parts and equipment for computers, telephones, and machinery.

7 India, especially Bangalore and Hyderabad, for information technology products.

8 Turkey for its sales of bakers' ovens and cheap retail goods to other Turkic-speaking peoples in the Balkans and Central Asia, and to Russia.

Pause in the search for more sales

9 Southern South America, especially Brazil and Argentina, needs to get its fiscal house in order, and Chile needs to get admitted to NAFTA sometime after 2003.

10 Central Europe, especially Poland, the Czech Republic, and Hungary, and the Baltic region, which need to get admitted to the EU between 2004 and 2010.

11 Russia and Ukraine, which need to deliver payments for all types of European-style goods.

No chance of being "hot" within the next few years

12 The Central Asian countries of the former Soviet Union need to invest their future oil revenues.

13 The Middle East, which needs to reduce the level of disputes among Israel, Palestine, and the other Arab states.

14 The Caribbean islands and the Andean countries of South America must shift some of their investments from commodities to higher value-added manufacturing.

15 Sub-Saharan Africa is condemned by population decline, lack of good infrastructure, bad government, and a host of calamities.

16 Iran needs to resolve the disconnect between traditionalists and reformers.

The best sales and marketing choices for international executives still are in the developed industrialized countries, especially those North American and European nation-states that are members of supra-national FTAs. Their membership in the FTAs gives firms the opportunity for scale and scope economies, sustainable competitive advantage, and above average returns. Of course, these will be the norm once the gloom and doom of 2001 is past.

ROLE OF MANAGERIAL DECISION MAKING IN INTERNATIONAL MARKETS

International managers can choose from a set of strategic alternatives, including product differentiation, new product design, and technological innovation, or focus on pricing and cost leadership. They can diversify across industries and product lines, or into new domestic and overseas markets. These executives can alter the value chain or the strategic activities of the firm. The crucial question for all firms remains as follows: Should they internalize all activities within the firm, or should they pay transactions costs to suppliers and other channel members, or should they do both? International business scholars label this the eclectic approach of international decision making under uncertainty.

Their boundaries for decision making are nation-states and the supra-national FTAs in North America, Europe, and elsewhere in the world. Each country has an industry structure that differs in large or small part from the industry structures of other nation-states. Also, each country places some roadblocks in the way of decisions, such as antitrust, anti-comparison ads, anti-price competition, use of government-owned infrastructure, etc. Moreover, each nation-state has a past history of strategic actions chosen and missed. Finally, both local government and business can and do get together to slow down the entry of new foreign competitors to contest local markets. Asymmetries in the information possessed by all players in a national market can make or break an investment decision by a foreign direct investor.

Let's turn our attention to the forward planning boundary set up by the European Union for business firms, and then compare and contrast it with what we know already about the boundary line set by NAFTA.

CASES: RYANAIR, GO, AND EASYJET

Management strategy

The UK management of low-cost flying from Stansted Airport to Edinburgh, Dublin, and Nice decided to have as few airline staff in the passenger cabin as the law from London and Brussels allows. This is the legal constraint on its no-frills, low-price strategy. These airline executives are using a backward induction process for their management strategy.

Then Ryanair, Go, and EasyJet set about making classless flying uncomfortable for everyone, not just in tourist class, so no one gets a meal or a drink on the plane. Instead, they offer lower, middle, and upper class passengers low prices. "We get the rich guys, who would normally fly business class for work, with their wives and kids. It can save them thousands of pounds," says Michael O'Leary, chief executive of Dublin-based Ryanair. The airlines' set of strategic actions is to help everyone in the population who wants to travel go somewhere every weekend.

Finally, these three low-cost airlines avoid the fixed-cost burdens of the network carriers by eliminating connecting services through hub airports, ending hotel beds for passengers whose flights are canceled, not providing free meals and drinks, which means the aircraft needs less cleaning, and not offering boarding passes. Tickets are sold over the Web using the latest in information technology. Theirs is a classic case of providing a service that many British and European consumers want. The three no-frills airlines have the growth in sales, increases in market share, and higher returns on investments to show for their low-price service.

Texas-based Southwest Airlines first started this type of service 27 years ago in the USA. It was good management strategy then in America, and it's good management strategy today in Europe.

CASES: ARM, AIZTRON, PROLION, FRESENIUS, AND JCB

Organization strategy

The management of US carmakers, Japanese electronics companies, and European manufacturers have to decide among a mix of "insourcing" and outsourcing strategies. For example, Arm from the UK is a "virtual" manufacturer of novel microchips used in telecommunications equipment. The firm does not make these chips. Instead, Arm licenses other firms to make chips from its own designs. Such outsourcing reduces the fixed costs of BT, Vodafone, Lucent, and NTT DoCoMo, and lets them focus on their core activities, such as design, marketing, and logistics.

Aiztron from Germany is the world's biggest manufacturer of machines for making complex compound semiconductors used in fiber optics, supermarket bar scanners, and electronic consumer goods. Moreover, Prolion from the Netherlands supplies robotic milking equipment for farms. They too outsource assembly, research, distribution, and marketing. Fresenius from Germany makes artificial kidney machines; it buys standard components for its machines, but makes its own pumps which are required for the crucial job of pushing blood around the machines as impurities are removed. Finally, JCB from the UK increased its production of hydraulic "rams" that power the buckets and scoops on its excavators, shifted "insourcing" from 70 to 90 percent of the rams, reduced its reliance on outside suppliers, and, as a consequence, employed its capital assets more productively.

All these European firms made choices about who does what in terms of manufacturing tasks, choices about in-process parts and final assembly, and decisions on product line variety, and substituting machines for people. The European Union's rules on country of origin permit outsourcing, programmable production, contract manufacturing, smart purchasing, pooling experience, and sharing ideas anywhere within the 15 nation-states that are members of the EU, and with those European countries, such as Switzerland and Norway, and other high-tech countries, such as Israel, with whom the EU has free trade agreements.

Given the size of the North American market under NAFTA, the opportunities for contract manufacturing in Mexico, and the potential for parts becoming commodities, European manufacturers compete in the following ways:

» Dominate product niches.
» Sell materials know-how and production skills.
» Build brand name recognition.

Example: Brembo of Italy colors its brakes Ferrari red so that drivers notice them in their cars.

» Lead in process technology.
» Tie-in suppliers.

Example: ASM Lithography of the Netherlands makes wafer steppers or machines that help make semiconductors, and buys its lens systems for these machines from its German partner, Carl Zeiss.

» Reduce prices occasionally.
» Employ mass customization.
» Add services.

Example: Heidelberger Druckmaschinen of Germany makes printing presses, and teaches printing techniques for customers in nine cities around the world.

"Insourcing" and outsourcing manufacturing are about how to use information technology. The crucial organization strategy is to link value chain activities within the firm and among suppliers via information networks, extract specific data and information, order components, and identify new e-business techniques. Jobs are allocated to contract manufacturers in Mexico, "virtual" manufacturers in the UK, and parts suppliers in Germany, the Netherlands, and Italy. When costs rise too fast in Mexico and in Germany some manufacturing is moved to China and to Poland. The name of the game is to produce parts and manufacture finished goods at the lowest cost possible anywhere in the world, and use sophisticated modern logistics to move these goods from point of production to point of consumption.

Of course, competitors from the developed world struggle and match lower costs, and, in turn, are replaced by other competitors from the emerging countries of Mexico and Latin America, Italy and southern Europe, and Singapore/Malaysia and South East Asia. These "hot" countries together with mainland China, India, Poland, and Turkey offer international executives a sharp sense of the limits of "insourcing," outsourcing, contract manufacturing, and final assembly of complex goods.

CASE: TESCO

Market strategy

The management of Tesco, a British supermarket chain, made important market decisions. For example, should the firm create a new channel of distribution for online retailing? Should it make this channel complex? Should the company invest in fancy conveyor belts, big warehouses, and cutting-edge computer systems?

Tesco did none of these things because it decided not to be all things to all people. It neither put up a glitzy Website nor spent millions on the latest distribution facilities. Instead, Tesco added a modest online delivery service to its traditional supermarket operation. Today, Tesco is profitable. It is ahead of Sainsbury as Britain's leading supermarket chain. Tesco is coming to the USA by helping Safeway compete against the Dutch supermarket, Ahold, as it improves the performance of its American supermarket chains, Stop & Shop, Giant Food, Bi-Lo, Giant Food Stores, and Tops Markets.

In summary, Tesco sees the Web as a new form of the mail-order catalog, or another channel of distribution that bricks-and-mortar supermarkets can tap. Its customers view the firm's Website as a new sales opportunity for obtaining the lowest price possible. Tesco gets vital customer information from the Web as shoppers browse and click product, pricing, promotion, and channel information. These data are fed back into decisions about products to keep in Tesco's inventory and to stock on the shelves of Tesco's supermarkets.

CASE: MSN EUROPE

Public strategy

The management of MSN Europe, Microsoft's Internet portal, acts as if there is no downturn in the dotcom, technology, and telecommunications sectors. In March 2001 MSN Europe over took Yahoo Europe as the most visited Internet site, and MSN is among the top five sites in all 15 nation-states of the EU. Now MSN is training its sights on its chief European competitor, AOL Time Warner.

MSN's products include Hotmail, the free e-mail service, Instant Messenger, and share portfolio and online photography tools. Of course, MSN amortizes the costs of development over 33 countries. MSN expects to make money selling advertising and merchandising over the Internet. Also, MSN wants to strike partnerships with Deutsche Telekom-controlled T-Online and Wanadoo of France because they dominate national ISPs. Finally, MSN needs to encourage users to part with their credit card information so that MSN can develop a billing relationship with its customers.

The battle lines are drawn between AOL's media and MSN's software. The former will have to contend with whatever the EU issues as directives to manage and protect competition within the media industry. To date, AOL Europe has no public strategy on this issue.

FTA STRATEGY

Here is a testable hypothesis: All the European firms discussed above might have done better in terms of sales, profits, and cash flow without the presence of the EU. The cases discussed above belie this statement. Thus let's draw the following conclusions:

» European firms carried out complex competitive strategies within the EU to contest local, national, and European-wide markets.
» Their EU strategy made it possible for the firm's managers to respond to changes in supra-national FTA rules, national legislation in key countries, and social and cultural values and lifestyles among all Europeans.
» These firms give attention to the need for neighboring countries to enter into FTAs and, once in, to gain a stable frontier for trade and investment analysis by international executives.

NAFTA AND THE EU

Before NAFTA and the EU, the nation-states involved in these two FTAs already had a high level of inter-regional trade among themselves. These two FTAs have been a great success. Both FTAs have increased trade and investment among the nation-states within NAFTA and those in the EU. The emerging and developed countries in both FTAs have become more prosperous. FTAs among neighboring countries that do a great deal of multilateral trade are a win-win global strategy.

SOURCES

Thorold Barker, "The woman who plans to beat AOL," *Financial Times*, September 5, 2001, p. 12.

Kevin Brown and Mark Odell, "A classless act," *Financial Times*, August 11/12, p. 7.

Daniel F. Spulber, "Economic analysis and management strategy: a survey continued," *Journal of Economics & Management Strategy*, 3:2 (Summer 1994): 355–406.

Victoria Griffith, "How the fittest survived the dotcom meltdown," *Financial Times*, August 27, 2001, p. 6.

Suzanne Kapner with Greg Winter, "The Dutch uncle of groceries," *The New York Times*, September 8, 2001, pp. B1–B2.

Peter Marsh, "How circuit boards generate serious profits," *Financial Times*, May 9, 2001, p. 13; "How to fight off your competitors," *Financial Times*, August 2, 2001, p. 10; "The intricate dance of the assembly line," *Financial Times*, August 1, 2001, p. 9; "Joined-up information," *Financial Times*, August 3, 2001, p. 8; "A sharp sense of the limits to outsourcing," *Financial Times*, July 31, 2001, p. 10.

Evolution

» Traces the development of global strategy from international trade and economics to foreign direct investment and international business.
» Examines the impact of organization, location, internalization, national character, and transaction costs on managing foreign investments under uncertainty.
» Presents free trade experiences in the United States and Mexico, Britain and Europe, and Japan.

Where did global strategy come from? How did global strategy reach the point where it is a crucial activity of global, multinational, multi-local, and domestic firms? Here are the significant milestones in the history of global strategy.

» **1870–1919**: Economists who study the comparative advantage of international trade take note of foreign direct investments by British-American Tobacco, Philips Electronics, and Bayern Aspirin in the USA. Bond rather than equity investments were the primary means for British and Dutch capital investments in building American and Canadian railroads in North America. Singer sewing machine, Colt revolver, and other US manufacturers set up "greenfield" factories in the UK; because Britain's Imperial Preference tariff schedule made export sales directly from England to Canada, Australia, and sub-Saharan Africa cheap, and from the USA to these same British colonies prohibitively expensive. Dunlop Rubber of the UK, Krupp Steel of Germany, and other European firms go into joint ventures with Japanese firms to help in the industrialization of Japan.

» **1920–1949**: Economists take note of foreign direct investments by General Motors and Ford in the UK and Germany, Unilever in China (Lux soap), and Philips and Nestlé in the US. Equity becomes the primary means for capital investment. German investments are seized as enemy war property after both world wars, and Japanese partners take complete control of investments in Japan.

» **1950–1969**: Economists declare American direct investments in western Europe, Canada, Mexico, Latin America, Japan, and South East Asia significant. However, they don't quite fit into theories about international trade (that is, comparative and absolute advantage), economic development (or the take-off in national income), international finance (that is, the foreign exchange value of national currencies), international marketing (or the 4 Ps of product, price, promotion, and place policies), and international management (that is, line and staff organizations). And these equity "greenfield" investments, acquisitions, and equity joint ventures became so large in volume and number that some economists opined that nation-states were powerless to stop multinational firms. Some said that this American challenge caused European sovereignty to be at bay.

» **1970–1989**: International business (IB) scholars come into their own with studies on how the European Common Market, the European Community, and, most recently, the European Union underpins nation-state sovereignty through supra-national FTAs. American-owned firms first and later European-owned firms began to manage European-wide manufacturing and distribution from their headquarters in London, Amsterdam-Rotterdam, Paris, or Frankfurt. During the 1970s and 1980s, IB scholars debate the importance of FTAs in Europe and North America and conclude that free trade is crucial to corporate success in northern and southern Europe, and in Canada and Mexico.

» **1990 to the present**: Today, IB scholars debate whether the corporate culture of parent firms should be or could be implanted overseas. Some suggest that one of the two following management strategies is better: Swiss, Dutch, and British openness versus American and Japanese closer control over foreign subsidiaries. These IB scholars together with some economists and marketers put these choices into the context of organization, market, and public policy strategies of multinational firms.

KEY LESSONS ABOUT GLOBAL STRATEGY

Here are the key lessons about global strategy from the cases discussed in the previous two chapters of the book:

1 In Chapter 1, global firms (for example, Swiss-owned Nestlé) pursue a global strategy in all world markets. Also, multinational firms (such as US-owned McDonald's, Belgian-owned Interbrew, and Japanese-owned Sony) implement both a global strategy in some world markets and a regional strategy in other world markets. Moreover, multi-local or multi-domestic firms (for example, Swedish-owned Ikea) follow both regional and local strategies in some markets overseas.

2 Within NAFTA, US-owned Wal-Mart (which itself is a muti-local firm) dominates the discount retail culture within Canada, the USA, and Mexico. Also, these three nation-states, together

through their FTA and individually with their own rules and regulations, set the boundaries for trade and investment decisions by Wal-Mart. Moreover, the cultural values and lifestyles among Americans, Canadians, and Mexicans help Wal-Mart determine the layout of stores, the assortment of merchandise, the prices charged, and promotion policies for stores in Toronto, Chicago, and Mexico City. Finally, Wal-Mart's adoption of complex competitive strategies prior to and after the adoption of NAFTA has led it to great success in North America.

3 In Chapter 2, all types of firms use backward induction to find out the legal boundaries set for them by nation-states and their supra-national FTAs, the EU and NAFTA. These regulations are the minimum number of cabin personnel on no-frills air flights within Europe. Also, the rules for contract manufacturing are the level and types of tariffs for suppliers, parts producers, and assemblers. Moreover, other legal procedures sort out the appropriateness of bricks-and-mortar retail buildings versus online retailing for the distribution of goods and services. Finally, competition laws affect the digital rollout of the media and telecommunications industries.

4 Chapters 1 and 2 rank the nation-states of the EU and NAFTA as "hot" countries for sales and marketing opportunities, especially in autos and auto parts, wired and wireless telecommunications, and other consumer and industrial goods. These are the key lessons about global strategy.

THEORIES ABOUT THE EFFECT OF NATIONAL CULTURE ON GLOBAL STRATEGIES

Here's what we know. Some countries are culturally close to the USA. These include Canada, the UK, and other English-speaking countries. Many are a bit more distant because of language differences, such as all the other 14 nation-states within the EU. Still others are culturally distant because of both language and levels of economic development, for example Mexico and many EU applicant countries from central and eastern Europe. Chapters 1 and 2 explain the cultural nearness and distance between the nation-states of NAFTA and EU, and the foreign-owned American, Mexican, Swiss, Dutch, British, and German investors in each of these countries.

Chapter 3 shows that some countries, such as Japan, are even more culturally distant from the USA. This is because of differences in language, levels of economic development, values and lifestyles, and government interaction with business firms. If international business (IB) scholars are correct in their collective interpretation of how national origin and cultural differences affect the strategies of multinational firms, then let's state what they believe are the obvious truths. Here are the two theories from IB scholars.

National character theory

Countries vary systematically in socio-cultural characteristics. These include the four classic dimensions of national culture:

1 Power distance is the extent to which individuals are comfortable with inequality in relationships.
2 Uncertainty avoidance, which is a tolerance for ambiguity.
3 Individualism is the extent to which individuals are expected to focus on their own needs and to solve their own problems.
4 Masculinity is the valuing of material possessions rather than relationships.

What are their relative strengths? Are these strengths relatively stable over time? How do they apply to Japan?

Of the four classic dimensions listed above, IB scholars conclude that Japan values only two of them highly. These are masculinity or material possession over relationships; and uncertainty avoidance or the ability to tolerate ambiguity. If IB scholars are correct, then Japanese executives are more likely to prefer wholly owned subsidiaries overseas because of the high level of the uncertainty involved in dealing with foreign partners from an equal or subordinate position.

Transaction cost theory

Cultural differences between home and the host countries bring about high market transaction costs. Hence, the purchase of know-how, raw materials, parts and components, and other goods in markets or through contracts is costly. Therefore, firms obtain these goods less expensively through equity joint ventures.

Is cost–benefit analysis stronger than the four classic cultural dimensions of national culture? Does this strength of cost–benefit analysis over the four cultural differences remain stable over time? How do these comparisons apply to Japan?

In terms of cost–benefit analysis, IB scholars conclude that Japan prefers to keep its new technology to itself because this is a strong competitive advantage. Japan will not share new information with outsiders unless this sharing is absolutely necessary. Here are some reasons for partnerships, alliances, and equity joint ventures.

First, Japan will pay consultants for market information about a market it does not know much about. Second, Japan will go into partnerships with foreign competitors to get to know their manufacturing and marketing practices, and then terminate the partnership after a decade or two. Third, if Japan needs some or all of a new technology, then it will consider licensing first, a short-time strategic alliance second, and an equity joint venture only as a last resort.

Let's temper these conclusions with the time-line of Japanese auto foreign direct investments in the USA.

- » Honda came first by acquiring idle auto plants without a local partner.
- » Toyota went into a joint venture with GM to learn more about the US market and GM as a competitor. Years later, Toyota set up its own "greenfield" investments in the USA.
- » Nissan set up its own plants both in the USA and in Mexico.
- » Mazda sold a third of itself to Ford. Then they worked together to set up shared manufacturing facilities in the USA. Also, Mazda built a plant for Ford in Mexico.
- » All Japanese transplants in North America import drive-trains and engines from Japan, and parts and components from Canada and Mexico.

Clearly, all Japanese multinational auto firms made their own decisions about costs and benefits. Some came to the USA alone; others sought out local partners for a while and then made other investments by themselves; and one sold itself to its US partner. Between the 1970s and the present, Japanese multinational auto firms became more comfortable with doing deals and making investments in the USA and within all three NAFTA countries. Over the past 30 years, the transaction costs came down for buying country-specific market information about the USA, and the know-how about parts and components technology from manufacturers in Canada, the USA, and Mexico.

However, Japan's national character intruded on this cost–benefit analysis, especially in the 1990s. Japan's understanding of the role of women in business is different than the social values, customs, and habits of women in business in the USA. Japanese auto multinational transplants learned some hard lessons about gender discrimination in the USA, and they had to pay compensation for this failure to understand the host country's cultural differences when it came to civil rights. This has required learning on the part of Japanese executives who work in the USA. In the first decade of the 21st century, the transaction costs for gender discrimination in the USA have not come down similar to the costs associated with technology and country-specific market information.

Conclusions

Professor John Dunning of the UK and author of the eclectic theory asserts that culture is central to international business research. Global, multinational, multi-local, and domestic firms identify and exploit cultural differences for their own competitive advantage in home and host countries.

Professors Jean-François Hennart of the University of Illinois at Urbana-Champaign and Jorma Larimo of the University of Vaasa conclude the following: Owing to national character or transactions costs or both, Japanese multinational firms across all industries have a lower preference for wholly owned subsidiaries and are more likely to enter the USA with joint ventures.

Professor Douglas Lamont of DePaul University concludes that the evidence from the Japanese auto transplants in the USA does not support the Hennart and Larimo conclusion.

Professors Tomasz Lenartow of The University of Texas at Austin and Kendall Roth of the University of South Carolina agree. They suggest that IB scholars put together valid cultural groups (e.g.,

Japanese auto executives in the USA) and do a cultural assessment of their social structures and collective behavior regarding their foreign direct investments in the USA. The core value of these transplant executives is to build up a Japanese auto industry in the USA that competes with the Big Two American-owned firms, GM and Ford, and the German-owned transplant firms, such as Daimler-Chrysler, Mercedes, and BMW. This core value among Japanese auto investors in the USA has been stable for almost 30 years. Although they pursue different approaches towards direct investments in the USA, they are harmonious in their collective will to build up Japanese auto transplants as strong competitors against other auto firms in the USA.

Professors Keith D. Brouthers of the University of East London and Lance Eliot Brouthers of the University of Texas at San Antonio refine this conclusion with the following points: Managers select partnerships, alliances, and equity joint ventures in culturally similar, low investment risk markets. Also, managers select wholly owned subsidiaries in culturally different, high investment risk markets. The problem with this conclusion is that Japanese auto transplants have selected both shared joint ventures and wholly owned subsidiaries as the means for foreign direct investments in the USA. Is the US market a low investment risk for some and a high investment risk for other Japanese investors? This does not seem probable. Was the US market low risk in the 1970s and 1980s and then high risk in the 1980s and 1990s or vice versa? The evidence from studies of Japanese auto investments in the USA does not underscore either of these two timelines.

Let's make the following conclusion: Japanese auto investors made a careful cost–benefit analysis of investment possibilities in the USA. They did not make their decisions based on whether the USA was a low- or high-risk investment opportunity. Nor did they make their decisions based on cultural differences between Japan as the home country and the USA as the host country. Japanese multinational auto firms acted in their own interest to build up sales and market share in the USA. This is their global business strategy.

FOREIGN DIRECT INVESTMENT

Case: country risk in Japan

Economic risk

After a decade of recession, Japan desperately needs investment from overseas. The Nikkei today is roughly two-thirds down from its peak in 1990. Japanese banks carry an estimated 70 trillion yen in bad loans. Government finances are approaching a state of collapse.

Cultural risk

However, without government help, many Japanese firms are attracting money from abroad. These are companies that list their stock abroad, e.g., as American Depository Receipts on the New York Stock Exchange, have English-language Web pages, and the willingness to take advice from foreigners through an official international advisory board.

Japanese restructuring (*risutoro*) includes permitting Renault's French executives to take over Nissan, and ending the descent from heaven of high government officials and former chief executive officers onto boards of directors as lifetime consultants. However, Japanese executives seem unable to make the following changes in their business practices:

» Start criticizing workers who are under-performing.
» End attending meetings in force as a courtesy even by those without data, information, and knowledge of the topics under discussion.
» Begin thrashing out points of differences with other executives and foreign partners in meetings even with the possibility of a loss of face.
» Speak Japanese without veiled courtesies and say "no" when you mean "no."
» Use English as the language of choice in official documents and meetings.
» Employ focus groups in which individuals criticize products and services.

- » Start self-promotion as lifetime employment ends for younger employees.
- » End rewards based on seniority for older employees.
- » Begin striking out alone as entrepreneurs.
- » Forget the loss of the "unique" Japanese spirit.
- » Use teams of women, and men and women who have worked overseas, to make waves within traditional Japanese firms.
- » Employ *sayonara* on tradition, ceremony, politeness, loss of face, etc.

American, Australian, and European executives are impatient with the snail's pace of change among Japanese executives. Yet today's haiku (a tiny, discrete poem of 17 syllables in three lines – of five, seven, and five syllables – in brief, elliptical, and often resigned sadness which deals in fine shadings of meanings, preferring gentle hints, and muted suggestions to anything stated plainly) salutes the west. Haiku is putting on a new suit of clothes from the wave of western art influences: symbols, naturalism, realism, etc. in which symbolic language from the USA plays an active role in breaking down the old rules of Japanese life.

However, some Japanese writers wonder whether the wearing of a western suit by Japanese executives is bad for Japan. They stress caution in trying to narrow the real differences between western and Japanese cultures. The latter's cultural history casts a long shadow across how Japanese business presents itself to the world, and to what extent Americans and other westerners come to believe – *mistakenly* – that Japanese values, habits, and customs are changing to meet the demands of partners and competitors from abroad. Therefore, don't undervalue cultural differences as the Japanese themselves did when they put on the clothes of Anglo-American liberal capitalism without regard to their non-Anglo-American tradition of social organization. This is the lesson of the decade- long recession in Japan.

Case: foreign auto investment in Japan

About one-half of Japan's total vehicle manufacturing is partly owned by foreigners. Here is an up-to-date list of the M&A deals made by American and European auto firms for Japanese auto companies.

In the later 1970s, the Sumitomo *keiretsu* sold 25 percent of Mazda, a money-losing auto firm, to Ford. Throughout the 1980s the two companies shared information, exchanged technical personnel, used some manufacturing and distribution facilities jointly, and, at the highest levels, played golf together. When Mazda needed manufacturing capacity in the USA, Ford helped it find space in Flat Rock, Michigan; when Ford ran short of US factory space, Mazda let Ford use the new facility; and when Ford needed a new small car plant in Mexico, Mazda built it for Ford. In 1996 Ford raised its stake in Mazda to 33.4 percent, which gave Ford control over this Japanese auto firm. In 2000 Mazda and Ford launched their first jointly produced, sports utility vehicle in the US market.

GM owns 49 percent of Isuzu, 10 percent of Suzuki, and 20 percent of Fuji Heavy Industries, the maker of Subaru cars. GM does not produce and sell its own cars in Japan. Instead, it depends on components and parts alliances with Isuzu, Suzuki, and Subaru in Japan and in much of East Asia. Moreover, GM spends its money exchanging engines with Honda, building new propulsion technologies with Toyota, and setting up an Internet-based marketplace with both Honda and Toyota.

Renault owns 36.8 percent of Nissan. Renault placed its own executive, Carlos Ghosn, in charge of Nissan. His task is to balance the interests of western investors, Japanese employees, and Japanese customers. Many Japanese customers agree with him that Nissan's models are bland and out of date, and they have left Nissan to buy cars from Toyota. Ghosn is out to cut costs and restructure Nissan's business in Japan. So far he has slashed 21,000 jobs, closed five factories, cut the number of suppliers in half, and imposed a new management discipline for Japanese executives. Ghosn has taken on the difficult task of changing Nissan's corporate culture.

For example, Ghosn created a network of nine cross-function teams that cover everything from design to purchasing to manufacturing, and which meet in Japan, Europe, and the USA. He broke down the territorial boundaries and the turf of Nissan's divisions. This is not a facelift, but a complete restructuring of Nissan. Ghosn introduced stock options based on worker achievement, and promotions based on performance. Ghosn's overall assignment is to overturn decades of Japanese corporate tradition.

Each foreign auto owner has acquired money-losing Japanese auto firms whose products have become dated and who have run out of money to make their car models competitive in Japan, in the USA, and in Europe. Through these acquisitions Ford, GM, and Renault gain control over Japanese auto plants in mainland China, South East Asia, India, Canada, the USA, Mexico, and Europe. These plants are being consolidated with the intention of having fewer Japanese auto plants and fewer manufacturing platforms throughout the world. About 50 percent of Japanese auto production is exported to the USA, Europe, and elsewhere in the world.

Since Japan harbors a national culture different than those found in the USA and Europe, many foreign auto companies will have more than the usual amount of difficulties with their Japanese acquisitions. Their formula for success with Japanese auto acquisitions remains elusive.

Case: *keiretsu*

Are the cooperative arrangements that bind banks, companies, and government together on their way out in Japan? These *keiretsu*, or powerful corporate groups, discuss closer business ties and ways to strengthen cooperation. They have common values, long-term business relationships, and a web of cross-shareholdings. Under the onslaught of Japan's ten-year recession, the acquisition of Japanese firms by foreign firms, the merger of Japan's big banks, and today's global recession, the *keiretsu* are falling apart. Hence the search by many Japanese auto companies for a new parent and partner from overseas.

Case: independent Japanese auto firms

Even though Honda and Toyota have alliances with GM over the exchange of engines and the development of propulsion technologies, these two major Japanese auto firms remain independent of both American and European auto firms. Nevertheless, both Toyota and Honda are part of Japan's accelerating industrial decline, surging levels of manufacturing unemployment, and sharp declines in consumer demand for cars in Japan, the USA, Europe, South East Asia, and Latin America. No market in 2001–2002 is exempt from the overall global slowdown and recessions in the industrialized world. These substantial declines in economic activity affect Tier I auto assemblers, and Tier II and III auto components and parts suppliers all over the world.

Nevertheless, the biggest Japanese auto firms, Toyota, Nissan, and Honda, are introducing new midsize models and sports utility vehicles in the USA that will compete on price, styling, and performance with similar models from GM, Ford, and Daimler-Chrysler. To survive the collapse of the Japanese home market, these three Japanese auto firms are striving to gain market share and dominant market categories in the US host country market. Time will tell whether their attack on the US auto market will succeed.

FTA strategy

Of course, Japan is not a member of a robust FTA, such as NAFTA and the EU. Along with virtually all countries that border the Pacific Ocean, Japan is a member of Asia Pacific Economic Consensus Group (or APEC) where presidents and prime ministers meet once a year to discuss trade and investment issues; they made one decision several years ago – that is, to reduce or eliminate tariffs on all manufactured goods traded among these nation-states by 2020. These tariffs are coming down slowly throughout APEC.

Also, Japan is the third largest trading partner of the USA after Canada and Mexico respectively. All Japanese-owned auto assembly plants that are located in these two North American countries can receive engines, transmissions, components, and parts from Japan and intermingle them with those similar products from elsewhere in North America. If 50 percent in value is added within one or more of the NAFTA countries, and the physical character of the components and parts is changed into finished cars (or substantial transformation), then the production from Japanese-owned plants is treated as if it is produced by US-owned plants in Canada, the USA, and Mexico. This then is the strategic response of Nissan, Toyota, and Honda to NAFTA in North America.

Here is a testable hypothesis: Japanese-owned auto firms might have done better in terms of sales, profits, and cash flow without the presence of NAFTA (and without the presence of the EU). The cases discussed above belie this statement. Thus let's draw the following conclusions:

» Japanese auto firms and their foreign partners carried out complex competitive strategies within NAFTA (and the EU).
» Their home country strategies made it possible for the firm's national and foreign managers to respond to changes in domestic economic

conditions, the role of *keiretsu*, and the evolving role of foreign firms in Japan's domestic economy.

» Their host country strategies made it possible for the firm's national and Japanese foreign managers to respond to changes in supra-national FTA rules, national legislation in key countries, and social and cultural values and lifestyles among North Americans and Europeans.

» Japanese auto firms give attention to the need for integrating Japan, as a neighboring country across the Pacific Ocean, into special trade and investment relationships with the three NAFTA countries, and other ties with the 15 EU nation-states.

SOURCES

Keith D. Brouthers and Lance Eliot Brouthers, "Explaining the national cultural distance paradox," *Journal of International Business Studies*, **32**:1 (First Quarter 2001): 177–180.

Tim Burt and Alexandra Harney, "'Le cost-killer' makes his move," *Financial Times*, November 9, 1999, p. 15.

John H. Dunning, "Micro and macro organizational aspects of MNE and MNE activity," in Brian Toyne and Douglas Nigh, *International Business: An Emerging Vision*, (Columbia, SC: University of South Carolina Press, 1997).

Masami Hayashi, ed., *One Hundred Contemporary Haiku for the Year Two Thousand*, (Tokyo, Japan: Gumma Prefectural Museum of Literature, 2001).

Jean-François Hennart and Jorma Larimo, "The impact of culture on the strategy of multinational enterprises: does national origin affect ownership decisions?" *Journal of International Business Studies*, **29**:3 (Third Quarter 1998): 515–538.

Douglas Lamont, *Global Marketing*, (Cambridge, Massachusetts: Blackwell Publishers, Ltd. 1996).

Tomasz Lenartow and Kendall Roth, "A framework for culture assessment," *Journal of International Business Studies*, **30**:4 (Fourth Quarter 1999): 781–798.

Piero Morosini, Scott Shane, and Harbir Singh, "National cultural distance and cross-border acquisition performance," *Journal of International Business Studies*, **29**:1 (First Quarter 1998); 137–158.

Norihiko Shirouzu, "GM cracks Japan market with its wallet, not its cars," *The Wall Street Journal*, January 26, 2000, p. A17.

Shirouzu, "Japanese car makers plan renewed assault on Detroit's family models," *The Wall Street Journal*, August 23, 2001, pp. B1, B6.

Emily Thornton, "Carload of trouble?" *Business Week*, March 27, 2000, pp. 56-57.

The E-Dimension

» Examines the importance of distinguishing the costs and benefits of intra- versus inter-firm supplier production networks.
» Considers the vital role that *keiretsu* played in Japan's global strategy and how lower cost options from mainland China are undercutting Japan's reliance on government–banking–industry partnerships.

Does global strategy need e-commerce? How do global, multinational, multi-local, and domestic firms apply bounded rationality and opportunism to global strategy? Here are eight action items for use in deepening the analysis of transaction cost theory as it affects the e-dimension of global strategy.

1 Use switching costs to determine source of competitive advantage.
2 Spell out the central role of asset specificity.
3 Determine the real boundaries of the firm within the global economy.
4 Purchase know-how, raw materials, and parts and components.
5 Execute contracts for suppliers and cost out make or buy decisions.
6 Integrate vertically through mergers and acquisitions of network members.
7 Form cooperative alliances among competitors.
8 Carry out a cost–benefit analysis on the firm's ideal and actual production, distribution, and marketing networks.

KEY LESSONS ABOUT THE E-DIMENSION

Here are the key lessons about putting the new economy of online production and distribution into the old economy businesses, such as the worldwide network of manufacturing factories, ocean shipping and air freight, and local assembly facilities for automobiles, computers, and consumer electronics:

1 Study intra-firm networks of parent firms and subsidiaries, and external contract networks of parts and components manufacturers, assemblers, and distributors. Compare and contrast the costs and benefits of in-house and external transactions. Decide on the boundaries of the firm and its overlap into the market.

2 Examine Japanese *keiretsu* as examples of where to set the boundaries of the firm. Prepare for opportunism as Japanese suppliers are replaced by suppliers from mainland China, Taiwan, and the countries of South East Asia. Calculate the cost of switching from older to newer sources of supply.

3 Create international trade and investment assets in mainland China under World Trade Organization (WTO) rules. Extend

export industries in soft goods, toys, shoes, automobiles, semi-conductors, computers, and information technology. Deepen import industries as China separates business from government, builds up fiber-optic networks, ends local-content rules, and protects foreign-owned intellectual property.

4 Recognize China as a strong competitor for market share in East Asia, the USA, and Europe. China together with the Chinese business tycoons who live and work in South East Asia have fostered a spectacular reproductive capacity for the repeated successes, failures, and successes in the China Commonwealth. China embodies the best and the worst of Asian values.

EAST-ASIAN SUPPLIER NETWORKS

For as many years as one can remember, Japanese suppliers have had a competitive advantage over other East Asian suppliers. Some of the former are subsidiaries and therefore a part of the intra-firm networks of auto, computer, and consumer electronics of Japanese companies; others are independently-owned Japanese firms, but are fully integrated into a *keiretsu*. None of these would think of switching from one *keiretsu* to another, because they would lose all financial and managerial support from their bank and cooperating Japanese firms.

These days are numbered because other suppliers in East Asia now can deliver the same chips, parts and components, and other assets at very competitive prices. Also, as mainland China joins the WTO in 2002, its ability to deliver a large domestic market to international firms becomes even more important than whether switching costs are slightly higher or lower than existing competitors, whether work is done within firms or transactions occur in markets, and the opportunity to deliver just-in-time inventory at competitive costs.

E-commerce gives assemblers of cars, computers, and consumer electronic goods the ability to buy from suppliers worldwide at the most competitive prices possible. Japanese *keiretsu* suppliers are vulnerable as competitors from China and elsewhere in East Asia deliver products of equal quality at lower landed costs. Production systems, fiber-optic networks, information technology, and the Internet carry the virus of the new economy into the global strategy of global, multinational, multi-local, and domestic firms. This is the e-dimension of global strategy.

Switching costs and competitive advantage

Global management strategy is a process of backward induction. New entrant firms may have higher production costs than incumbent firms because the latter benefit from learning by doing. In this case, incumbents have a competitive advantage. Also, incumbent firms might decide to keep prices up because they have locked-in customers. This too is a competitive advantage for incumbents.

However, new entrants might lower prices to encourage customers to switch. Then both sets of firms might aggressively engage in price competition for market share. Or they might not. Here is the crucial question: If new entrants use lower prices to attract high-demand customers, will incumbents follow suit with lower prices or will they keep their prices up to retain only the low-demand customers? If incumbents choose the latter course, then switching costs make incumbents less aggressive in competition with new entrants. Over time, this becomes a competitive advantage for new entrants.

Here's what we know. Incumbents firms may be forced to fight large-scale entrants while finding it more profitable to accommodate small-scale ones. Some incumbents, particularly those that face new large-scale entrants who have different and superior technology, may want to avoid a knockout; these incumbent firms might even terminate suppliers, close factories, reduce market output, cut sales commitments, and get out of specific national markets. Either incumbents or new entrants or both may gain competitive advantage.

Intangible assets and international diversification

Both incumbent and new entrant firms do cost–benefit analyses, use switching costs to gain competitive advantage, and make within the firm or buy in the market parts and components, in-process and finished goods, and services and capital. In the mid-1980s, as the world negotiated the latest round of multilateral trade negotiations that led to the setting up of the World Trade Organization (WTO), the term globalization came into its own. This meant a surge in foreign direct investment (FDI); most of it was in capital- and technology-intensive sectors of the economy. From the mid-1980s to the mid-1990s, the dominance of FDI by the Organization for Economic and Cooperative Development (OECD) countries of Europe, the USA, and Japan began to include non-OECD and non-WTO countries of East Asia, especially mainland China as the host country, and some South East Asia countries as home countries, such as Singapore and Taiwan.

By the mid-1990s, trade and investment are linked. Both have become essential to global, multinational, and multi-local firms for effective market access. These firms gain scale and scope economies, customize products to satisfy consumer tastes, establish high-quality internal and external corporate networks, and acquire technology, managerial skills, and market knowledge.

About 25 percent of exports worldwide are intra-firm (that is, between the parent firm and its subsidiaries, and among subsidiaries of the same firm). Also, 50 percent of US exports and 60 percent of US imports are within one multinational firm. If licensing, franchising, and royalty fees are added to these totals, then 80 percent of US foreign trade is linked closely to one single business firm in the USA. Most of this intra-firm trade is in the form of intermediate goods, and this shows the growth of tightly managed vertical and horizontal network links within the firm's value-added chain.

Global, multinational, and multi-local firms made impressive strides in building a single global market for parts and components, supplies, semi-finished and finished goods, and services and capital. This was the past.

E-commerce

Today, multinational firms are rolling out electronic commerce on the Internet. Since the Web has low entry barriers for information-related services, e-commerce will change the structure of certain sectors of business. Small and medium-sized firms will use switching costs to build up asset specificity and become competitors to the bigger firms.

Case: Japanese auto firms

In Chapter 3, Japanese auto investors make a careful cost–benefit analysis of their investment opportunities in the USA. Instead of switching to new suppliers who are American- or Canadian-owned, Japanese-owned Tier I assemblers preferred to keep their home country supplier networks intact and demanded they send Tier II and III parts and components to their plants in Ohio, Illinois, Kentucky, Ontario, and Aguascalientes, Mexico. Included in their analysis of switching costs were the additional costs of ocean and air freight, tariffs, domestic rail and truck service, and all the mistakes made in the name of just-in-time inventory. Once the auto factories were settled pieces of the American manufacturing fabric, they set up their supplier networks on the Mexican side of the US border to begin lowering costs in the face of stronger national competition from US-owned Tier II and III suppliers.

The real boundaries of Japanese auto firms include the production and sales of cars in Japan, North America, Europe, Latin America, and elsewhere in the world. These factories exchange vehicles, models, and parts and components through intra-firm transactions within the multi-local boundaries of the auto firm, and through contracts with suppliers, parts providers, and other network members. Fickle customers force Japanese auto makers to be more flexible in what they manufacture at their quick-response assembly plants for the home and host country markets. Their task is to gain scale economies faster than their American and European counterparts.

Case: cost-saving strategy of just-in-time inventory

Fully assembled cars and other large industrial equipment come from Japan and Europe to the USA by ocean shipping. The cars are driven onto the ships at their points of embarkation, put in the hold, and then driven off the ships at their points of disembarkation in Los Angeles and Baltimore. The sailing time is 12 to 14 days from Japan to the West Coast of the USA.

Parts and components come to the USA by air freight. Half the goods moving by air across the Pacific are shipped on planes shared with passengers. Much of that traffic is in electronic products and components – microchips headed from the USA to assembly plants in Taiwan, China, and elsewhere, and completed cars, computers, digital assistants, phones, and other products making the return trip. AMD ships wafers from plants in Austin, Texas, Germany, and Japan to assembly and test sites in Singapore, Malaysia, Thailand, and China. Dell

Computer Corporation has 7 to 10 days' worth of inventory in the USA. Just-in-time inventory is the cost-saving strategy for auto, computer, and other manufacturers.

Mainland China is experiencing a silicon rush as foreigners and Chinese alike race to set up factories that make, assemble, or design chips for computers, mobile phones, and every other electronic device. New plants are being built in Tianjin, Shanghai, and elsewhere on the mainland. China has a pent-up demand for chips with a growth rate of 20 percent annually. New uses in China include telematics in cars and trucks, smart toys, and other appliances. Also, China has an abundance of engineers who come from a competitive elite that may be better than those trained in Japan, and their salaries are a quarter to one-third of their Japanese colleagues'. Moreover, Shanghai has an abundance of clean water and a stable electricity grid. And unlike Taiwan, Shanghai does not straddle an earthquake fault. Finally, the real problem in China is weak protection of intellectual property, which will hurt smaller chip manufacturers. When China joins the WTO the country will begin doing a better job of protecting this property under the new TRIPS code.

Yesterday, China made soft goods and consumer electronics for itself and for the world. Tomorrow, China will make chips for itself, and, one day, for the world.

ASIAN VALUES

Before July 1997 and the crash of several East Asian currencies, Japan, South Korea, Singapore, Taiwan, Hong Kong, Malaysia, Thailand, and China were considered miracle countries. Then, one by one, these countries stalled and some of their national economies collapsed. By 2000 a few had begun to recover and then the US economy stalled. Two-fifths of all information technology exports from East Asia had gone to the USA, and now these had ended. *Sic transit gloria*.

Here are a few reasons why East Asia went down. First, the countries lack transparency in balance sheets, income statements, bank records, and accounting reviews. Second, they lack good corporate governance by independent boards of directors. Third, the countries lack careful legal protection by securities commissions, attorneys general, and courts of law. Within East Asia, there is an absence of proper checks and balances by local governments, public markets, and minority shareholders to monitor the crony capitalists who descend from government heaven in Japan to be corporate consultants, the friends and families of party members in China, and the well-connected *huaqiao* (or tycoons from the ethnic Chinese minorities) in South East Asia.

Historically, all of these cronies expropriate the interests of foreigners over time. Instead, they are internalized within the family, the party, the family or party firm, and the bamboo network of Chinese interests both inside and outside China. These crony capitalists practice Confucian values of hierarchy, authority, and loyalty; they invest quickly based on gut instinct, do business with other *huaqiao*, and seal their deals with their word and not with written contracts. These Chinese ventures have layers and layers of holding companies, subsidiaries, cross-holdings, and informal links.

In summary, these Chinese firms have done as much as possible to internalize business functions rather than doing transactions in the market. This world is over. The e-dimension of global strategy will make both state- and privately-owned firms, their equity joint ventures with foreign-owned firms, and all other business deals more transparent to all in and outside China.

CHINA AS COMPETITOR

Recognize China as a competitor against Japan, the countries of South East Asia, and India for market share in the USA, Japan, and Europe. Let's rank-order the elements of country risk: economic, political, business, financial, and cultural risks. Continued high levels of foreign direct investment strengthen China's national economy. These will continue to grow so long as the domestic politics of China show more transparency, and the joint ventures with well-placed family members of party officials conform to the rules of the WTO. The worries of other East Asian countries suggest that the Chinese market, with socialist characteristics, has indeed become a regional economic colossus.

Country risk

During the 1980s, China created a market economy with socialist characteristics. China followed its East Asian neighbors into export markets in the USA; textile and clothing, toys, and shoes were the leading exports at prices a great deal lower than those from Japan, Korea, Taiwan, Singapore, and Thailand. Also, China allowed foreign direct investments into southern and coastal China first, then Manchuria, and finally into the "third ring" cities of rural China; foreign investors had to have local joint venture partners from government-owned state enterprises and well-connected private firms that are owned by party officials and their families.

After 20 years of great success and some setbacks, China entered the 21st century with its newest corporate culture:

» intra-firm networks, equity joint ventures, and other boundary extensions of the firm;
» higher value-added products with imported technology for domestic use and export sales;
» pricing strategies to encourage switching from higher-cost Japanese *keiretsu* products to lower-cost Shanghai-Pudong goods; and
» management of just-in-time inventory as US, European, and Japanese firms seek further international diversification.

Clearly, China has become a manufacturing colossus. Although China has wide disparities of wealth, two-fifths of its residents now own their own homes. Within the next 20 years, China expects to become a "middle income" country with an income per capita equal to South Korea or Portugal.

Foreign direct investment

China's stock of foreign direct investment (US $350 billion) ranks third after the United States (US $1.1 trillion) and the United Kingdom (US $394 billion). China's FDI is far ahead of Mexico and Brazil. Four-fifths of all FDI going to South East and East Asia, not counting Japan, is sucked up by China. The other countries of the region see China as a major threat in trade and investment. Today, the following multinational and multi-local firms dominate some sectors in China: McDonald's, Kentucky Fried Chicken, Kodak, Fuji, Procter & Gamble, Motorola, Ericsson, Nokia, and Coca-Cola.

Joint ventures

Today, when western firms set up their Chinese holding companies and buy into existing state-owned enterprises, the former get the latter's Chinese supervisors and plant staff, too. "All these [Chinese] joint ventures are unhappy in more or less the same way." Americans view their Chinese partners as hardworking, but unable to make decisions without checking with higher-ups. Chinese view their American partners as condescending and unyielding in their approach to workplace issues. According to the Chinese, these foreigners know little about China. They are all short-timers in China because they are afraid of being forgotten by their parent firms in the US.

FTA strategy

Of course, China is not a member of a robust FTA. China is a member of APEC, and together with other Asian and Pacific members China has agreed to eliminate tariffs on manufactured goods traded among these nation-states. China is the third largest recipient of foreign direct investment from Japanese, American, and European multinational firms. Some of these local Chinese equity joint ventures are playing a new role within the production and distribution networks of parent firms. As the boundaries of multinational and multi-local firms broaden out to include the market transactions between parent firms in the USA and Europe and Chinese equity joint ventures, China works on switching production from internal, intra-firm arrangements (so-called internalization) to external, inter-firm contracts with transactions in the market. Since China is not a member of an FTA, some Chinese firms have moved their textile and clothing production to Mexico to take advantage of free trade with the US under NAFTA.

Here is a testable hypothesis: Chinese equity joint ventures might have done better in terms of sales, profits, and cash flow without the presence of NAFTA (and without the presence of the EU). The cases discussed above belie this statement. Let's draw the following conclusions:

» Chinese equity joint ventures are beginning to carry out complex competitive strategies within China, East Asia, in North America, and within NAFTA (and the EU).

» Their home country strategies made it possible for the firm's local managers to respond to changes in domestic and foreign economic conditions, and the role of intra-firm agreements and inter-firm contracts to build up Chinese contacts in the world economy.

» Their host country strategies are just beginning with limited foreign direct investments in one NAFTA country, Mexico, and for one business reason – that is, to get Chinese exports into the USA without tariffs and quotas.

» Chinese equity joint ventures give attention to the need for integrating China into special trade and investment relationships with North America through the WTO and NAFTA.

E-BUSINESS

Today, successful firms are using e-business to leverage the new infrastructure and applications of the Internet. They are learning to do electronic procurement, production, distribution, and e-customer relationship management. These give them a tangible market advantage.

The Chinese equity joint ventures have been faster out of the gate to learn about the ever-changing nature of e-commerce than have the Japanese *keiretsu*. The Chinese together with the Americans are learning about price transparency, electronic markets, knowledge management, supplier network applications, and e-project pitfalls.

Technology

Investors have spent a fortune on installing networking technologies. There is now a vast over-capacity. Yet eventually the capacity will be used, often for purposes never foreseen when it was installed just a year or two ago. In the long run, the Chinese-American connection will be better for it. Of course, the Japanese-American connection will have to make a choice: compete or fall behind. The answer to this question is unknown at this writing.

English will remain the dominant language of the Internet. Chinese will come in a close second. Japanese is non-existent on the Internet. Both Americans and Chinese use the Internet, the Web, and e-mail for business and personal use; the Japanese are way behind in their adoption of these new technologies and ways of doing business. Unless the Japanese move quickly to reassert themselves through an up-to-date network of intra- and inter-firm (market-based) transactions, they will fall behind the Chinese from the mainland, Taiwan, Hong Kong, and in South East Asia.

Forecast

Chinese equity joint venture deals will replace Japanese investment arrangements as the main focus of international business in the next few years. Global strategy needs to get ready for an upheaval in the way in which scholars look at it and how business executives carry it out.

SOURCES

"China's economic power: enter the dragon," *The Economist*, March 10, 2001, pp. 23–25.

"A giant sucking sound," *The Economist*, December 2, 2000, p. 63.

Rahul Jacob, "Plumbing the depths of mutual disdain," *Financial Times*, March 28, 2001, p. 11.

Mark Landler with Richard A. Oppel Jr., "Ban on airliners' freight has businesses scrambling," *The New York Times*, September 15, 2001, A18.

Sylvia Ostry, "Technology, productivity and the multinational enterprise," *Journal of International Business Studies*, 29:1 (First Quarter 1998): 85–99.

Norihiko Shirouzu, "Fickle consumers force auto makers to be more flexible," *The Wall Street Journal*, September 10, 2001, p. B8.

"A survey of Asian business: in praise of rules," *The Economist*, April 7, 2001, pages 1–17.

Rugu Wang and Quan Wen, "Strategic invasion in markets with switching costs," *Journal of Economics & Management Strategy*, 7:4 (Winter 1998): 521–549.

The Global Dimension

» Global strategy succeeds when free trade agreements (FTAs) turn nation-states and prosperous regions into brand names.
» Examines the skills used by Mexico in pushing itself ahead of its Latin American rivals in the quest for market share in the neighboring United States.
» Considers the difficulties of creating value-based strategies within emerging countries that are culturally distant from developed countries.

What are the implications of globalization?

» Countries and their regions are brands.
» Nation-states (and regions) are heterogeneous in terms of their policies on trade and investment.
» Free trade agreements between developed and emerging countries enhance the brand image of the latter countries and their regions.
» FTAs change the economics of intra-firm, internal, non-market agreements *vis-à-vis* inter-firm, external market contracts.

KEY LESSONS ABOUT THE GLOBAL DIMENSION

1 Some FTAs have a positive stock of brand capital. NAFTA is a good example. The USA is a member of the G3, and both the USA and Canada are members of the G7. These two countries have a good brand image because of their mass market of 300 million consumers who share similar values, habits, and lifestyles. On the other hand, one member, Mexico, is seeking to enhance its brand image by moving itself closer to its two NAFTA partners. Other Latin American countries say simply: "Mexico has made it!"

   Their multinational and multi-local firms share in this good brand image. Examples include: McDonald's, Coca-Cola, Gillette, IBM, Procter & Gamble, Colgate, Motorola, Wal-Mart, Microsoft, Warner Brothers, Six Flags, 7-11, Costco, AT&T Broadband, Levi's, GM, and Citibank from the USA; Molson and Macmillan Bloedel from Canada; and Cemex and Bimbo from Mexico.

2 The poorer regions of the European Union draw closer to their richer counterparts through incentives and other experience goods. The west of Ireland, the south of Spain, the *Mezzogiorno* of southern Italy, and the eastern region of Germany receive special grants and aid from the EU and their respective nation-states. Altogether these 15 countries have a good brand image because of their mass market of 400 million consumers who share the "potato" lifestyles of northern Europe and the "spaghetti" customs of southern Europe. When new members from central and eastern Europe are admitted to the EU, they

too will be known among Europeans as countries that "have made it!"

Their global, multinational, and multi-local firms share similar experience goods. Examples include: Nokia, Ericsson, KPN, Ikea, Mercedes, Tesco, Minitel, Manchester United, Nestlé, Philips, Royal Dutch Shell, ABB, Siemens, Vivendi, Sanpaolo Life, Unilever, Renault, Interbrew, and Ryanair.

3 FTAs play a part in determining which suppliers, firms, and buyers make up value chains. Japanese firms prefer intra-firm or internal arrangements, such as *keiretsu*, and will move only reluctantly to inter-firm or external market contracts. Add to this the opportunity cost of not doing anything as FTAs establish themselves as lower-cost alternatives for supply parts, semi-finished, and assembled goods from Mexico to the USA or from the poorer regions to the richer areas of Europe.

Their multinational and multi-local firms share similar questions about value chains. Examples include: Toyota, Honda, Nissan, NTT DoCoMo, Sony, Fast Retailing, Yamaha, and Sanyo.

4 Mexico has played a skillful game in pushing itself ahead of peers in Latin America and raising itself up to higher levels of competition with the USA, Canada, Europe, and elsewhere in the world. Mexico (and especially the Mexican north) has become the entrepot for trade and investment between North America and the rest of the world. Mexico's multi-local firms, Cemex and Bimbo, have become stronger competitors in the USA and throughout the world.

NATION-STATES AS BRANDS

The global economy has a stock of well-established nation-states, a stock termed brand capital. Let's divide them into three groups.

The free trade areas (FTA) with the greatest capital are the European Union (EU) and North American Free Trade Area (NAFTA). Other countries with a similar amount of brand capital are Japan, China, South Korea, some nations in South East Asia, India, and Turkey.

These are the nations in which business executives look for sales and marketing opportunities.

The FTAs with more limited capital are the Common Market for southern South America (Mercosur) and the Association of South East Asian Nations (Asean). Other countries with the same amount of limited capital are future members of the EU from central and eastern Europe and Russia. These are the nations in which business should pause in the search for more sales.

The FTAs with even less capital are the Caribbean Basin Initiative, Andean nations customs union, and the Southern African Development Group. Other countries with little brand capital are Iran, and the countries of the Middle East, Central Asia and sub-Saharan Africa. These are the nations for which no chance of large-scale sales exists within the next few years.

Nation-states with the greatest brand capital are able to introduce new trade and investment opportunities for multinational and multi-local firms. These are in response to information about new technology and new products, the transaction costs inherent in inter-firm production networks, and the growth in sales and marketing opportunities. The most successful countries do these things before rival nation-states. Also, the best play a better competitive game than the latter in terms of opening markets, delivering good prices for enhanced quality, and making accurate forecasts about the future.

Brand capital is the source of heterogeneity among nation-states. Some are called G3, G7, industrialized, developed first world countries. Others are emerging third world, less developed, poorer nations. A few of these will break out of their relative poverty and make it into the developed world. Many others are highly in debt and remain poor. These differences among countries are the distinguishing characteristic of globalization today.

Trade and investment

Nation-states with high values of brand capital are most likely to do more foreign trade and receive higher levels of foreign direct investment, such as the USA, the UK, and most recently China. Those with lower values, such as Mexico and Brazil, receive fewer good foreign trade deals and lower levels of FDI. Also, countries with high values of brand capital have a stock of organizational capital, such as superior market information, lower costs, and deeper use of FTAs. This resource-based view of nation-states falls into the theory of national character.

The nations with high values of brand capital are the first to gain market share overseas, to build up high levels of interregional trade with neighboring countries, and create successful FTAs in select regions of the world. Of course, brand capital relies on an asymmetry among nation-states in their ability to induce locally- and foreign-owned firms to introduce new technologies, products, and strategies. Under the rules of the FTAs and the WTO, the countries and their local incumbent firms are unable to deter the entry of foreign-owned multinational and multi-local new entrant firms.

Brand image

Within NAFTA, the USA and Canada have an image of openness. On the other hand, Mexico faces an image cost for its past economic performance, its present-day wage and fringe payments and lower levels of productivity, and future breakdowns in telecommunications and transportation infrastructure. As Mexico has committed itself to free trade with the USA under NAFTA for over seven years, Mexico's brand image has improved to the point where Japanese, Korean, Chinese, German, and British multinational firms set up their factories in Mexico for delivery of goods in the USA and Canada. Mexico has moved away from its original brand image of a poor, less developed country to one of an emerging, more prosperous nation-state. American consumers think less of Mexico's country-of-origin and more of its ability to deliver quality products at competitive prices. Within NAFTA, Mexico has an incentive to build its brand image up to be as close as it can to the image prevalent in the USA and Canada. Hence, both the Mexican government and its business firms must invest in building up the capacity for change, growth, and image.

Experience goods

All foreign direct investments in countries new to firms are experience goods for these investors. They discount the utility of investments in nations they have not tried before, and they seek local government incentives to make these investments happen on a timely basis.

Nation-states do make mistakes. They might introduce a bad brand image because they are required by local politics to induce multinational private investment in their poorer regions. However, if these same countries looked at their less-developed regions as product line extensions, then the west of Ireland, the south of Spain, the *Mezzogiorno* of southern Italy, and the eastern region of Germany might just obtain the same brand image as the country as a whole.

Of course, the size of the discount decreases with increasing closeness of the region and the new country to previous investments by multinational firms. This is true in the Fos region of southern France and the Lille region of northern France as both reduce their differences with the rest of industrial France. No doubt, without the intervention of the French government, incumbent strongholds, such as Lyons and Besançon, might have taken a pre-emptive strike against the entry of new competitive regions within France.

Organizational strategy

Therefore, global organizational strategy links suppliers, contract manufacturers, parts producers, and assemblers via data and information networks to local, regional, and national governments. All of them share information about where to locate and how much to invest in any given period. Global organization strategy requires multinational and multi-local firms to be on the lookout for low-cost opportunities and to put these in play so governments can determine their response in terms of incentives. Opportunism is one of the great levelers in today's global economy.

Value chain

The value chain includes three categories of players – suppliers, firms, and buyers. How much value do all players capture? What is their individual positive added value? How does a player create favorable asymmetries between itself and other firms in the value chain? Are the firms adopting an external focus – one that is oriented towards the buyers they serve and the suppliers they rely upon?

The situations within value chains are unstructured because each value chain has a different combination of intra- and inter-firm cooperative arrangements and market-based contracts. A mix exists in which some supplies are shipped through channels controlled by the firm and in which other goods are sold through independent distribution channels. These are scope economies. Heterogeneity exists among value chains. Hence, suppliers, firms, and buyers interact with one another on a free-form basis, and each value chain offers the market different forms of added value. This is called value created.

Here is a to-do list:

» Buyers acquire goods free of charge because they are part of the intra-firm channel. These are internal to the firm. They are non-market arrangements. IB scholars call these deals internalization. They expand the legal, management, organizational, and market boundaries of the firm.
» Buyers pay for these goods because they are part of the inter-firm channel. These are external to the firm. They are market contracts. IB scholars call these transactions. They too expand the legal, management, organizational, and market boundaries of the firm.

As noted in the Japanese cases, their auto, computer, and consumer electronics firms prefer intra-firm or internal arrangements within the *keiretsu*. Suppliers, the firms, and buyers incur very high switching costs to shift from one intra-firm non-market arrangement to another or to inter-firm market transactions. Japanese public policy is against suppliers, firms, and buyers changing their allegiance from one *keiretsu* to another. Only in extreme cases in which one member is losing money or going bankrupt does the Sumitomo Bank sell Mazda to Ford.

These same value chains incur only slightly higher switching costs to shift from one inter-firm market contract to another, especially to those whose suppliers are in a lower-cost country, such as China, the countries of South East Asia, and Mexico. Although the market price might be slightly lower, members of the value chain incur opportunity costs when they forsake the known for the unknown channel of distribution.

FTAs

If Japanese firms abandon their Japanese-based suppliers for another group of firms in mainland China or Thailand, the firms obtain lower costs but they still must pay tariffs when their goods are shipped to the USA. If these same firms use suppliers in Mexico, the firms get both lower costs and tariff-free access to the US home market. In this case, Mexico is a better choice (that is, the opportunity costs are favorable) for those Japanese firms whose buyers are in the USA. Japanese firms learn to deal with approbation of their home country peers and government with the sure knowledge that as first movers into Mexico they will get a leg-up on long-term growth in sales and increases in profits.

Mexico has a strong bargaining position *vis-à-vis* the East Asian countries because of its position as a founding member of NAFTA. Today, Mexico is becoming a tough bargainer as its government under President Vincente Fox seeks to position itself as the world's entrepot for free trade. Mexico now has free trade agreements with three big markets – North America, the European Union, and Latin America (through individual agreements with Chile, Colombia, Venezuela, Bolivia, Costa Rica, Uruguay, and Nicaragua). Mexico has become the hub and its partners the spokes for free trade.

Mexico's agreement with the EU reduces tariffs on all industrial goods and eliminates them completely by 2007. Also banking, insurance, and other services are liberalized. Only agriculture and farm products are not part of Mexico's free trade ties with the EU. Moreover, Mexican products will not face tariffs in Europe while comparable American goods will have to pay tariffs to Brussels. The same rules apply to Latin America. Therefore, Mexico becomes the location of choice for both intra-firm and inter-firm supplier networks for Europe, Latin America, and the USA.

The USA needs to negotiate a free trade agreement with the European Union and some or all of the Latin American countries to negate Mexico's current competitive advantage. In short, FTAs must be a major part of global strategy.

Value-based strategies

Since brands and images make countries heterogeneous, their public policy strategy becomes crucial to the success or failure of nation-states as hosts for export–import trade and foreign direct investments. Nation-states must have positive added value and be different from their competitors. This means that countries must have a favorable asymmetry between themselves and other nation-states.

Mexico has created a home market for itself that includes itself, the USA and Canada. Its decision offers transferable utility to Mexican- and US-owned firms. Both Cemex and Bimbo enjoy broader and deeper trade and investment opportunities today than they had in the pre-NAFTA period. Also, Wal-Mart and other US-owned firms have created a home market for themselves that includes all three NAFTA countries. The micro boundaries of these firms and the macro boundaries of the FTA have been extended far beyond what is generally recognized in the strategy literature.

FTAs assign results to multinational and multi-local firms, their value chains, and internal and external networks of suppliers, producers, and distributors. Firms make decisions. Governments make decisions. Together, they bargain among themselves to promote free trade with neighbors, friends, and allies. Some governments get ahead and gain first-mover advantage, and drive their advantage at home by broadening and deepening their commitments to free trade.

These business episodes have been especially important for Mexico. It has pushed itself ahead of its Latin American peers and it has raised itself to new levels of competitiveness with the USA. Mexico has captured more value than all other nations in Latin America. Mexico's new role is the direct effect of globalization.

GLOBALIZATION

Economic performance of firms depends on social resources that the firms do not themselves create. Firms are social networks as well as networks of intra-firm arrangements and inter-firm contracts. Firms that use the same technologies and produce the same products differ systematically across societies, nations, regions, cities, towns, and villages.

For example, Mexico has a comparative institutional advantage that builds on its long history of economic woe *vis-a-vis* the USA and its more recent adoption of its neighbor's ideas about free trade. Japan has a comparative advantage that shows the world that economic development can occur within two generations and economy recovery can occur within one generation. Italian regions have a comparative institutional advantage that shows local people can do the job of macro- and microeconomics with or without the states. To date, all three varieties of capitalism are resilient equally in an open international economy.

Nation-states may be stable. Regions and local towns are continuous and stable over long periods of time. They should not be dismissed in the quest to explain global strategy by global, multinational, multi-local, and domestic firms within the EU, NAFTA, and other free trade agreements. Instead, IB scholars need to see that the different responses to globalization by regions within nation-states reflect deep and enduring forms of economic and business behavior.

Regions within nations

IB scholars use nations as the basic unit of analysis and they seek to explain cross-border variation in economic performance by focusing on particular FTA, and other, trade and investment arrangements. They are driven to this destination because data, such as the gross domestic product, are collected on a national basis. The gross regional product is hard to calculate.

Notwithstanding these data problems, observers can see that the Mexican north has pushed itself ahead of its peers in central and southern Mexico, and the Mexican north has raised itself to new levels of competitiveness with the American South and Southwest. These new levels of productivity, job creation, higher incomes, and middle class lifestyles are evident all along Mexico's border with the USA. All of the border factories (*maquiladoras*) are tied into both intra- and inter-firm supplier networks for the production of cars, computers, and consumer electronics by US, Japanese, Korean, German, and other foreign-owned multinational and multi-local firms. These border plants use numerical control machines and other sophisticated computer-controlled equipment, and they employ a well-trained Mexican workforce. The Mexican north is a new region of prosperity in North America.

Case: Reggio Emilia

Italy has an even more pronounced internal heterogeneity within its national economy. Economic, industrial, and marketing activities are embedded within local socio-economic networks. Italian regions have a quality of life, a respect for traditional values, a sense of belonging to a community, and the value of solidarity absent from thoughts about the Italian nation-state. These regional characteristics help companies adjust successfully to changing world markets. Their human capital can sense and believe in the future.

In Reggio Emilia, a northern town about 1½ hours from Milan, small firms are part of larger inter-firm networks. These smaller Italian firms are ahead of the larger British firms in terms of total value added. The former produce machine tools, specialty steels, textiles, apparel, fashion and design, ceramic tiles, and specialized mechanics. Regio Emilia has one of Italy's highest gross products per capita, and also leads Italy in terms of economic growth and exports.

The town is known for its cheese, Parmigiano Reggiano. It is also the headquarters for Max Mara, a fashion company and global leader in high-class ready-to-wear clothes. Reggio Emilia is home to Fantuzzi-Reggiane, a global market leader in the manufacture of transport equipment from lift-trucks to cranes; Interpump, a manu-facturer of high-pressure plunger pumps and cleaning equipment; and Comer, the largest manufacturer of gearboxes and drivelines for agricultural equipment in the world. All of these firms are high-tech without being directly involved in information and communication technology.

Regions as brands

Each region within Italy has a distinctive brand image. They deliver a heterogeneous set of experience goods. Their organizational strategy is to be successful locally, offer the market positive reasons for direct investment, and make sure their firms carry out value-based strategies. All regions within Italy benefit from the EU because it gives them a much larger home market.

Here is a testable hypothesis: Italian small firms might have done better in terms of sales, profits, and cash flow without the presence of the EU. The cases discussed above belie this statement. Let's draw the following conclusions:

» Small and medium-size Italian firms are carrying out complex compet-itive strategies within Italy, the EU, and elsewhere in the world.

» Their home regional strategies made it possible for local managers to respond to changes in domestic and foreign economic conditions.
» Their host country strategies are to export larger quantities of goods to the rest of Europe and overseas.
» Small Italian firms from Reggio Emilia give attention to the need for boosting regions and offering them help to create brand capital.

Forecast

Small Italian firms from Reggio Emilia and other Italian regions will dominate the Italian economy for the foreseeable future. Global-regional strategy needs to get ready for an upheaval in the way in which scholars look at it and how business executives carry it out.

SOURCES

Suzanne Berger and Richard M. Locke, "*Il Caso Italiano* and globalization," in "Italy: Resilient and Vulnerable, Volume II: Politics and Society," *Daedalus*, 130:3 (Summer 2001): 85–104.

Adam M. Brandenburger and Harborne W. Stuart, Jr., "Value-based business strategy," *Journal of Economics & Management Strategy*, 5:1 (Spring 1996): 5–24.

Alessandro Cavalli, "Reflections on political culture and the 'Italian national character,'" in "Italy: Resilient and Vulnerable, Volume II: Politics and Society," *Daedalus*, 130:3 (Summer 2001): 105–118.

Robert M. Dunn, Jr., "Mexico's fast start on free trade," *The New York Times*, July 5, 2001, p. A20.

Douglas Lamont, *Managing Foreign Investments in Southern Italy*, (New York: Praeger Publishers, Inc., 1973).

Louis A. Thomas, "Brand capital and entry order," *Journal of Economics & Management Strategy*, 5:1 (Spring 1996): 107–129.

The State of the Art

» Global strategy favors geographic nearness over distance between nation-states.
» Global strategy prefers cultural similarities over distance among countries.
» Global strategy accepts cultural distance when administrative and economic distance is narrowed through FTAs.
» Nation-states as heterogeneous agents with choices to make about incentives for trade, investment, and alliances.
» Switching costs for firms when they change location of factories.

Let's review the current debate over global strategy. The following are the most important questions that are being debated about global strategy:

» Why is global strategy important?
» How do business firms choose among global-regional strategies?
» What is the impact of national culture on global strategy?
» Which countries have brand name recognition?
» What is the impact of free trade agreements?

The answers to these five questions explain a great deal about where global strategy has been and where it is going in the future. Current debate among international business strategists raises the question of one country's cultural, administrative, geographic, and economic (or CAGE) distance from another, and the answer shows their impact individually and collectively on different products and industries, foreign trade and direct investment, and free trade agreements. Let's do three things. First, show how nearness and distance affect global strategy. Second, use the CAGE distance framework prepared by Pankaj Ghemawat of Harvard University, and review the countries discussed in Chapters 1 through 5, and show why some of them and other countries will not make it in the global economy of 2001–2002.

KEY LESSON: NEARNESS OVER DISTANCE DETERMINES TRADE AND INVESTMENT

1 Global strategy favors geographic nearness over distance among countries, especially between nation-states that share a common border, such as Canada, the USA, and Mexico, or France, Germany, and the Benelux countries.
2 Global strategy prefers cultural similarities over distance among countries, especially between English-speaking countries, such as Canada, the USA, and the UK, or advanced western European nations.
3 Global strategy accepts cultural distance when administrative and economic distance are narrowed through FTAs, high levels of trade and investment by multinational and multi-local firms,

and joint work towards opening more sectors of the economy, such as arrangements to lower US and EU barriers across the North Atlantic.

4 Global strategy struggles to succeed when all four attributes of distance (that is, cultural, administrative, geographic, and economic) put trade and investment deals in jeopardy when firms determine how different most East Asian countries are as their economies slow, recessions begin, and structural impediments grind up even good quality firms.

5 Global strategy comes up with a new decision-making tool for international business strategists. Since no average developed country and no average emerging nation-states exist for IB firms, the latter now recognize heterogeneity among nation-states. The best-managed multinational firms put together a new foreign direct investment program (or at least rework an older program) that can be applied to the new environment for global business. These choice models estimate the demand for new investment opportunities in countries at a distance from the mass markets of the USA and the EU. Although Latin America, South Asia, the Middle East, and sub-Saharan Africa all aspire to IB greatness, they will not get the investment they desire because multinational firms will deepen their NAFTA and EU commitments first and then try to salvage their East Asian deals. This is the game plan for 2001 and 2002 while the US and global economies are slowing down and, perhaps, going into a prolonged recession.

AMONG THE NAFTA COUNTRIES

Case: Canada and the USA are siblings

Cultural

By law, Canada is a bilingual country with almost 80 percent of the population speaking English and the other 20 percent speaking French. Its immigrant population comes from former British and French colonies in South and East Asia, the Caribbean, and sub-Saharan Africa. By common consent, the USA is a monolingual English-speaking country. Its immigrant population comes from many places, but so much of it comes from Mexico and Latin America that nearly 15 percent of the population speak Spanish with a limited knowledge of English. Therefore, some cultural distance exists between Canada and the USA, especially to protect Canada's English-speaking (or Anglophone) population from becoming too American.

Canada insists products sold nationally have bilingual labels and use the metric system of weights and measures. Wal-Mart has learned to do these things successfully, and puts Canadian products into US distribution. Also, Canada protects its cultural industries, such as TV, radio, magazines, and newspapers. However, fast food, Hollywood movies, professional sports, executive personnel, MBA training, and many other things of the good life in North America are similar or the same. Therefore, Canada as a brand name is widely recognized among Americans, Europeans, and others worldwide. "Canada has made it!"

A contrary view about cultural distance

Shawna O'Grady of Queen's University and Henry W. Lane of the University of Western Ontario studied Canadian retailers in the USA and concluded that these foreign business executives did not find it easy to manage their operations in the USA. The reason: These retailers assumed cultural similarities, did not learn about critical differences, and hence failed. Their conclusion: Familiarity breeds carelessness. The authors call this the psychic distance paradox. They suggest managerial competence requires a deeper understanding of the differences between American and Canadian retail business cultures.

The other CAGE distance attributes are relatively unimportant for global strategy in terms of trade and investment with Canada:

» *Administrative.* The national governments of Canada and the USA dispute timber and milk subsidies, cod and salmon catches, and whether to pipe petroleum and natural gas from Alaska, through Canada, to the United States.
» *Geographic.* Canada shares a common border. It has integrated its transportation, communication, finance, business, police, and military with the USA.

» *Economic*. Canada has slightly higher costs of doing business and marginally lower consumer incomes.

Case: Mexico and the USA are second cousins

Cultural

By law, Mexico is a monolingual, Spanish-speaking country with almost 10 percent of the population who live in southern Mexico speaking native Indian languages. The educated elite speak English, too. It is predominantly Roman Catholic with a small and growing Evangelical Protestant minority. Mexico is a country of the night for music, fiestas, and fireworks while the USA is a country for daytime 24/7 work and recreation.

Administrative

Mexico lost one-half its territory in a war with the USA. Mexico is a unitary state with taxes collected and distributed by its government in Mexico City. The national governments of Mexico and the USA dispute sugar subsidies, environmental rules, and whether to offer cabotage for the trucks of both nations

Geographic

Mexico shares a common border. It has not integrated its transportation, communication, finance, business, police, and military with the USA.

Economic

Mexico exports its unskilled poor people to work in the field, factories, and restaurants of the USA. The costs of doing business with the Mexican government bureaucracy are higher; however, Mexico's labor costs are one-seventh of those in the USA.

Mexico prefers Spanish language content on packages and in ads, hot salsa content in its food, traditional *ranchera* music, firms as national champions, low-value-added products, and many other differences from the North American norm. Both McDonald's and Wal-Mart in Mexico, and Cemex and Bimbo in the USA have narrowed economic distance between Mexico and the USA. Moreover, NAFTA has brought Mexico closer to the USA in terms of the administrative and economic attributes of the CAGE framework. Therefore, Mexico as a brand name is widely recognized among Americans, some Europeans, and several nationalities from Asia. "Mexico has made it!"

ACROSS THE NORTH ATLANTIC

Special case: the UK and USA as first cousins

Cultural

By common consent, the United Kingdom is a monolingual, English-speaking country with small numbers of people who speak an older Celtic language in Wales. The country is predominantly Protestant with an established state church in England and a large Roman Catholic minority all over the UK. Its immigrant population reflects people from the former colonies of Great Britain. The UK shares with the USA similar tastes in music (for example, opera, the Proms, rock), murder mysteries and Booker Prize fiction, movies, and many other entertainment spectaculars. Tesco's preference for the old economy in retailing with some attributes of the new economy is crossing the ocean to Safeway in the USA.

The UK and the USA share colonization of the latter by British subjects, revolutionary war and choice of allegiance between Crown and Republic, the division of North America between the USA and Canada, differences over southern disunion, British investment in US railroads and industries, two world wars, and the Korean and Gulf Wars. About 50 percent of the US population claims ties of generations to English, Scottish, Welsh, and Protestant Irish immigrants, and another 20-30 percent claim one or more ancestors from the British Isles, or grandparents who served in the Canadian and American forces in southern England before D-Day in June 1944. Thus the British and Americans are "kissing" cousins who always make up after small disputes, such as the Suez War of 1956.

Administrative

The UK has been a unitary state for almost 300 years centered in London, England, with a current policy of devolution to Scotland and Wales. Its disputes with the USA are those of the European Union over antitrust rules and banana subsidies.

Geographic

The UK is across an ocean and does not share a common border with the USA. However, its communication, finance, business, police, and military work closely with the USA, but landing rights (or "Four Freedoms") at international airports are in dispute.

Economic

The UK shares a preference for market economies with a bit more government involvement than in the USA. The UK's trade and investment decisions are circumscribed by the EU.

The UK shows that geographic distance does not matter much when there is slight cultural distance between two English-speaking countries. Therefore, England (as Americans call the UK) is a brand name widely recognized among Americans, continental Europeans, and most people around the world. "The UK has made it!"

AMONG THE EU COUNTRIES

Case: the 15 friends and acquaintances of the EU

Of course, the European Union is a work in progress. Its 15 member nation-states are close in terms of geographic distance (for example, France and Germany, or the three Benelux countries). Through the work of Brussels and other political organs of the EU, these member states are narrowing some of their administrative and economic distance. Their peoples share higher standards of living and costs as the value-added tax is collected to pay for trade, labor, and social welfare programs of the EU. Of course, all 15 countries and their internal regions present many and varied cultural differences. For example, England prefers America's English-speaking business culture, but wants continental Europe's month-long vacations in northern Italy or the south of France. France abhors the USA's business culture, but wants to push its national champion firms into worldwide dominance. And Italy depends on its regions (such as Reggio Emilia) to be successful as a national economy with the EU.

Most western European nations share consumer and corporate cultures with the USA, Canada, and the UK. Some southern, central, and eastern European nations do not share all the attributes of these cultures with the USA and the UK. In these cases, all four distance attributes of the CAGE framework do affect global strategy of global, multinational, and multi-local firms from the USA, the UK, and some countries of continental Europe. Thus Americans recognize the EU as a quality brand name and its member countries receive the same affirmation of quality on a collective basis. Also, Americans see individual quality within each member nation for Unilever and Tesco of the UK, Philips of the Netherlands, Danone of France, Siemens of Germany, ABB of Sweden, Nokia of Finland, Merloni of Italy, etc.

Therefore, ''The EU has made it!'' And some of the member countries have made it, too!

ACROSS INTO ASIA AND THE PACIFIC

Case: Asian strangers for the USA and the EU

No doubt Japan, mainland China, and the other countries of East Asia are where distance still matters. Let's use the CAGE framework once again. Check off the differences:

- » *Cultural.* History. Language. Ethnic backgrounds. Religions. Social norms. Products must be country-specific with an easy identification to the nation.
- » *Administrative.* Colony. Defeat. Occupation. Currency. *Keiretsu.* Communist party. National champions. Infrastructure.
- » *Geographic.* Far away from mass market. Size of population. Climate.
- » *Economic.* Consumer income. Natural resources. Infrastructure. Human resources. Knowledge. Business systems. Personal relationships.

Notwithstanding these differences, until 1991 Japan was in the running to displace the USA as the most important world economy. Then it faltered, slipped, and fell into a deep and long-standing recession. Korea, Taiwan, Hong Kong, and the South East Asian countries used exports of high- and low-tech products to take over Japan's place. In 1997 they too faltered, slipped, and fell into deep recession. Now, through no fault of their own, the USA has gone down, and they are laying off people, ending new home sales, and closing down their export-oriented economies. Mainland China still sees itself on an uptick, but the numbers on the rate of annual economic growth may be exaggerated, and China may suffer the same consequences.

Thus the CAGE framework warns about exaggerating the attractiveness of foreign markets, especially in East Asia, and suggests how to avoid expensive trade and investment mistakes. The CAGE framework does not provide foreign business investors with the warning lights from the USA slowing down, Japan going into a decade-long recession, and Europe failing to redo its government-laden labor, social welfare, and fiscal and tax markets. These too are important as investors with limited capital choose nearness over distance in their trade and investment decisions.

Although international business strategists thought Japan, Korea, Taiwan, Hong Kong, the South East counties, and, perhaps, mainland China had made it, the reality is different. Their brand logos lack the instant recognition that they are successful economies today. "Japan and the others have *not* made it!"

REST OF THE WORLD

Case: The sad state of neighbors, friends, and acquaintances

Brazil, Argentina, and the rest of Latin America may envy Mexico's geographic nearness and slightly less cultural, administrative, and economic distance with the USA. Their common market (Mercosur), customs union (Andean Pact), and free trade agreements (CACM and CBI) work in fits and starts. Not even a Free Trade Agreement of the Americas (FTAA) can turn most Latin American and Caribbean nations into a new Mexico.

Brazil

Brazil struggles to preserve its national identity within Mercosur, the FTAA, and the global economy. Its size makes it a large continental country similar to the USA, Russia, China, and India. Brazil dominates all other countries in South America. Its population is 160 million. Brazil has a GDP of over US $700 billion and it is the seventh largest economy in the world. Brazil's heterogeneity includes the three affluent southern states with a largely European population, the industrial center of São Paulo and nearby industrial states, the poverty of the northeast, and the vast openness of the isolated Amazon Basin. Brazil's commitment to the Mercosur customs union expresses its vision of open regionalism in which the modernization agendas of Brazil, Argentina, and other southern cone countries are made compatible with one another. Many multinational firms invest in Brazil because their global strategy would be incomplete without a foothold in Latin America's largest economy. Although Brazil exports Embraer planes, Busscar truck platforms, and RSB media ventures, Brazilian firms are virtually absent from the making of foreign direct investments in non-Mercosur countries.

India

India belongs to no FTA. Its population is one billion with nine-tenths of the people Hindu and one-tenth Moslem. Western (especially British and American) intellectual images of India see cultural uniformity among the chaos and poverty on the sub-continent. However, business executives view India's heterogeneity among the cities of New Delhi, Mumbai (Bombay), Calcutta, Chennai (Madras), Bangalore, Hyderabad, and many others; they deal with many different languages through multiple ad campaigns across the country. Many British, American, and Japanese multinational firms invest in India because their global strategy would be incomplete without a foothold in South Asia's largest economy. Although Bangalore exports information technology and Bollywood movies, Tata and other Indian firms are largely absent from the making of foreign direct investments in both the developed and emerging countries.

Turkey

Turkey wants to belong to EU and might be asked to join in about ten years once it becomes more European and secular, and less Middle Eastern and radical Moslem. This means once the ancient Saint Sofia Church of the Greeks, turned into the Aya Sofya mosque in 1453 by the Ottoman conquest, is returned to the Greeks for religious services by their Patriarch. Virtually everyone today is Moslem, even in Europe's largest city, bustling Istanbul (from which all but 2,000 Greeks have fled their beloved Constantinople for Greece itself while the Kurds from eastern Turkey have taken over the big Greek-owned houses in the Fenar). What once was a mosaic of differences – cultural, religions, linguistic, geographic, and political – has become Turkish. Clearly, modern-day Turkey draws inspiration from western liberal models through which the west redefined Turkey as a transit zone for ships, railroads, telegraphs, and oil. Turkey and the Middle East always have been a zone of unsettled identities, of constant quests that now produce resurgent religions, especially radical Islam, and antagonistic politics among the mullahs, military, bureaucracy, business elite, and the democratic option of the growing middle class.

South Africa

South Africa is "a Belgium within an India ... A dual economy with a high-skill, capital-intensive modern sector alongside a mass of unskilled people scratching a living from subsistence farming, casual employment and self-employment." South Africa is lucky with the quality of its domestic institutions (that is, a free press, independent judiciary, churches, trade unions, non-governmental organizations, and a well-developed and socially engaged business community), and its choices of economic policies towards tariff reductions, capital flows, the transfer of knowledge, low inflation, affordable budget deficits, secure property rights, and efficient and non-corrupt governance. South Africa used to produce all the tradable goods (except oil, minerals, and commodities) for southern, central, and East Africa, while Nigeria did the same for West Africa. Today, these two sub-Saharan countries compete for market share within Africa.

Diversity

Brazil and Latin America; India and South Asia; Turkey, and the Balkans and the Middle East; and South Africa and sub-Saharan Africa: All are different. Most think they want free trade and investment links to Mercosur, Asean and APEC, the EU, and even to NAFTA, but few want to make the sacrifices that free trade demands. Remember: FTAs work well only when high levels of inter-regional trade exist previously among member states. Hence, the great success of NAFTA and the EU, and the more modest success of Asean, Mercosur, and the apparent failures of the Andean Pact, CACM, CBI, and other FTAs.

No brand names

Don't expect any new investments in foods, textile fibers, sugar and honey, and fertilizers. These are highly sensitive to distance. Perhaps, these countries might promote new investments in cork and wood, footwear, watches, and office machines. These are less sensitive to distance. However, as the global and the US economy slows, and the EU and Japanese economies slow down even further, look for multinational and multi-local firms to choose investments in nearby markets over those in distant markets. Unfortunately, Brazil, India, Turkey, and South Africa do not have a sufficient set of multinational and multi-local firms to compete effectively against similar firms from the USA, UK, Europe, and Japan. Therefore, the former have no brand names among their set of nation-states worthy of the phrase "They made it!" in today's global economy.

NATION-STATES AS HETEROGENEOUS AGENTS

Case: heterogeneous countries

Developed countries

Let's recall our fundamental conclusion. Although we speak of developed countries, no average developed country exists. The USA is light years different from Canada. The USA has scale, with 270 million people, most of whom participate in the mass market. Also, it is the home of many multinational and multi-local "Fortune 500" firms. Canada has 31 million people, a smaller-scale mass market, and one that is heavily dependent on foreign direct investment by US firms.

Also, the USA is not the EU. The former is monolingual with one national culture. The latter is multilingual and with many national cultures. Although the EU has a total mass market of over 400 million people, it is divided by northern and southern food and lifestyle choices, wider income disparities, and a symphony of many languages. Also, the EU is bisected by wide regional divisions within its 15 member states. Moreover, the EU is the home of some global, and many multinational and multi-local "Fortune 500" firms. Finally, the EU is dependent on foreign direct investment by US firms.

Of course, neither the USA nor the EU is Japan. The latter has a total mass market of 120 million people; however, many Japanese couples are not replacing themselves and immigration is not widely accepted; thus the Japanese population is expected to decline. Also, the Japanese economy is in deep and long-term recession. Since many are unemployed, they are not spending their funds on consumer goods. Without sales, Japanese firms are not investing in new plant and equipment. The only Japanese firms that seem to be surviving are those that take on a foreign partner with new funds and new managerial talent who set out to change the way the Japanese firms do business.

These then are the developed countries on three continents. Each is different in its own right. They are heterogeneous. Thus IB firms must devise different global trade and investment strategies to make money in North America, Europe, and Japan.

Emerging countries

Let's restate our fundamental conclusion. No average emerging country exists. Mexico is light years different than all other emerging countries. The country is within NAFTA and has free access to the US market. No other emerging country has this significant free trade benefit with a developed country.

If and when Poland, the Czech Republic, and Hungary get into the EU, then they too will be light years ahead of all other emerging central and eastern European countries. Within the EU they will have free access to the European market. This will be a significant free trade benefit.

Similar to the three central European countries mentioned above, all the emerging countries in East and South East Asia have substantial language, religious, and other cultural differences, and economic and administrative differences. These nations are also distant from the mass markets of the USA and the EU.

Of course, the countries of Latin America, South Asia, the Middle East, and sub-Saharan Africa are all heterogeneous. Without country-specific investment plans IB firms will not be successful in the emerging, third-world, less developed countries. Thus firms must make choices.

Choice models

IB scholars report on the regularity of diversity and heterogeneity among nation-states and the different trade and investment choices made by firms. The recognition of this heterogeneity has had profound consequences for the applied economic theory about international business and for the economic practice of IB executives in the global economy.

IB scholars answer the following policy questions:

1 *Treatment effect*: What is the effect of an incentive program, such as subsidizing plant and equipment expenditures, to bring new foreign direct investment into a region or a nation? Is the result the same on new and existing foreign investors? Will established investors add to their existing plant and equipment? Will non-investors change their mind and make new investments? Would an alternative incentive program, such as tax rebates on profits earned, bring more new investors into a region or a nation?

2 *Structural estimation*: What is the effect of a completely new program, such as trying to attract larger foreign-owned firms to Reggio Emilia, on a traditional older, highly successful program, such as supporting linkages among locally owned, small and mid-size firms? If the EU reduces subsidies to the regions of Italy to pay for subsidies to the regions of Poland, how would this change in the environment of public subsidies affect the search for larger foreign investors or the support for linkages among smaller local firms or both?

The public policy of supranational FTAs and national (and regional) governments demands their offices of trade and investments do something about the unfavorable conditions that put a region in disfavor among foreign investors. For example, the region labeled Poland-A is favored by foreign investors because it is near the German border, whereas Poland-B (which the Poles themselves derisively call Asia) is not favored by foreign investors because it is east of Warsaw near the Belarus–Ukraine border. The government cannot give away the factories in Poland-B because they lack good road and telecommunications connections with the rest of Poland and the EU. Also, the government cannot get foreign investors into the factories because the machinery and equipment are out of date and the local working population lacks the requisite skills to be competitive in the Polish, EU, and global economies. In terms of treatment effects, the Polish government might do just as well by doing nothing because no set of incentive programs will make multinational and multi-local firms choose this region over a better region within Poland, or choose to go into eastern Germany and enjoy the benefits of the EU.

Of course, once Poland is in the EU it can petition for special regional grants-in-aid – that is, if these funds have not been committed to western Ireland, southern Spain, and *Il Mezzogiorno* Italy. In this case, Poland needs to make a structural estimation of this new program on the new environment of both Poland-A and Poland-B within the EU.

Switching costs

Business firms incur switching costs when changing from one region to another, or one country to another. These include the costs of learning about the new government, new local partners, and the new linkages in transportation and telecommunications. Nations and their regions charge different prices to existing and new foreign investors. For example, Mexico and its Pacific Coast region paid Ford to switch small-car production from the American Midwest to Hermosillo in northern Mexico. This is a form of third-degree price discrimination. Market outcomes, such as staying in the Midwest, moving to the American south, or going to Canada, differ under different forms of price competition. Given that Mexico is more desperate for higher value-added jobs, its regional foreign investment program (or Secofi) offered more and better incentives than Illinois, Tennessee, or Ontario. Hence, the global strategy of Ford is to maximize the incentives it receives before it builds its auto assembly plant in Mexico. Given the three countries are in NAFTA together and this FTA permits using government incentives to encourage switching by investors, Mexico can offer as many incentives as it can afford to foreign investors.

Mexico acts as a heterogeneous agent for business executives who need to make choices about their foreign direct investments. The countries of Latin America, South Asia, the Middle East, and sub-Saharan Africa will have to do the same or fail to get new investments from foreign-owned multinational and multi-local firms. This is a tall order for them. The die has been cast to favor northern Mexico within NAFTA and Poland-A once it is inside the EU.

Here is a testable hypothesis: Nation-states might have done better in terms of more foreign trade and direct investment by offering the same incentives to all existing and new investors. The cases discussed above belie this statement. Let's draw the following conclusions:

» Developed industrial countries offer investors diversity and heterogeneity in the size of mass markets, income disparities, high levels of inter-regional trade, lifestyle choices, and linkages to neighboring and distant countries.

» Less-developed emerging countries offer investors diversity and heterogeneity in the robustness of middle class markets, income disparities, lower levels of inter-regional trade, choices between western and local lifestyles, and transparent linkages to export markets among the developed countries.

» The variety of home and host country strategies among developed countries and the variety of host country strategies among emerging countries determine the switching cost of incentives for foreign investment.

» Some emerging countries will try to offer deeper price discounts on investments than Mexico without understanding Mexico's true competitive advantage: NAFTA, geographic nearness, less cultural and economic distance, and the same administrative distance.

Forecast

Nations and regions will offer multinational firms a wider array of incentives because they need to create jobs for local citizens. Global-regional strategy needs to be ready to review these incentives and decide which terms to accept and which to reject. This is the work of business executives.

SOURCES

Leslie Boyd, Michael Spicer, and Gavin Keeton, "Economic scenarios for South Africa: a business perspective," in "Why South Africa matters," *Daedalus*, 130-1 (Winter 2001): 71–98.

Yongmin Chen, "Paying customers to switch," *Journal of Economics and Management Strategy*, 6:4 (Winter 1997): 877–897.

Pankaj Ghemawat, "Distance still matters: the hard reality of global expansion," *Harvard Business Review*, 79:8 (September 2001): 137–147.

James Heckman, "Micro data, heterogeneity, and the evaluation of public policy: Nobel lecture," *Journal of Political Economy,* 109:4 (2001): 673–748.

Martin Kramer, "The Middle East, old and new," in "Human diversity," *Daedalus,* 126:2 (Spring 1997): 89–112.

Celso Lafer, "Brazilian international identity and foreign policy: past, present, and future," in "Brazil: burden of the past: promise of the future," *Daedalus*, 129:2 (Spring 2000): 207–238.

Shawna O'Grady and Henry W. Lane, "The psychic distance paradox," *Journal of International Business Studies*, 27:2 (Second Quarter 1996): 309–333.

Amartya Sen, "Indian traditions and the western imagination," in "Human diversity," *Daedalus,* 126:2 (Spring 1997): 1–26.

In Practice: Global Strategy Success Stories

» Wide selection of cases about nation-states and business firms as strategists from Mexico, the United States, Canada, Europe, and India.

Global strategy is about two crucial ideas:

» Countries present heterogeneous characteristics in the world market.
» Business firms develop global strategies based on these differences.

KEY LESSONS ABOUT THE STATE AS STRATEGIST

Countries make choices about their role in the world market. Some choose to join free trade agreements (FTAs); others prefer to go it alone. Some offer investment incentives to multinational firms; others do not. These are two examples of the state as strategist. Here are a few lessons.

1 Successful countries present more positive than negative hetero-geneous characteristics in the world market. For example, they are members of FTAs. Also, "hot" nation-states perform tradi-tional trade and investment activities differently – e.g., support exports with less-than-market interest rates, or waive corporate taxes for up to ten years. Moreover, these successful countries decide to go into the international market with a different set of economic activities than their rival countries – e.g., offer free trade in goods, capital, services, and even in labor. Thus nation-states must make choices about the role of domestic and foreign-owned business firms in furthering free trade goals.

2 "Hot" nation-states make trade-offs among preferences for domes-tic control, the middle-ground option of partnerships and allian-ces, and the difficulties of foreign ownership, especially in steel, autos, airlines, and energy. For example, successful countries push privatization for state-owned enterprises. Or they keep some sectors under limited state control, but insist they compete against private firms in both domestic and export markets. Also, these "hot" countries encourage either intra- or inter-firm trade and investment networks or both among their domestic and foreign-owned firms. Thus as nation-states seek more foreign trade and direct investment, they must position themselves to take advantage of the cultural, administrative, geographic, and economic (CAGE) attributes of distance in global strategy.

KEY LESSONS ABOUT THE FIRM AS STRATEGIST

1 International business scholars proclaim organization, location, and internalization (OLI) as the eclectic paradigm, or the theory from which nation-states and business firms prepare a global strategy.

2 Since nation-states display a wide diversity and substantial heterogeneous behavior, international business executives must be able to discern these differences and prepare export and direct investment strategies accordingly.

3 When nations deliberately decide to join FTAs, IB executives have a new set of trade and investment activities from which to deliver a new mix of socio-economic value to their local employees, host and home country shareholders, and citizens at large. Mexico inside NAFTA, for example, permits foreign investors to offer better, higher-paying jobs and improved social welfare benefits to Mexican citizens. Also, Mexico inside NAFTA offers domestic Mexican-owned and multinational firms free trade in goods and capital with the USA. Moreover, since Mexico chose to subsidize new foreign direct investments, multinational and multi-local firms obtain incentives for using existing plant and equipment, no tariffs on the import of new machinery, cuts in welfare costs, and tax rebates on profits. Thus Mexico's deal with the USA attracts tariff-sensitive firms from Europe, China, and India that otherwise would ship products across the oceans with a great deal of uncertainty about entry into the USA.

4 In the cases of northern Mexico's leading-edge auto industry cluster versus Ontario, Canada's auto cluster, the former receives more new investors and a great deal of the new investment funds for expanding US- and Japanese-owned auto parts and components, and assembly facilities. Therefore, the Mexican state as a global strategist did a better job of providing for and selling its inducements and incentives to multinational executives than the Canadian state and the local American state governments in the Midwest.

5 Tacit knowledge about technology and managerial competence tends to be embedded internally within the firm. The parent firm must transfer knowledge effectively to its subsidiaries, or send them out into the market to buy alternative technology. In many industries, especially in the auto sector, the latter strategy is a non-starter because of the uniqueness of engine, transmissions, and other technologies within the firm.

6 Many overseas subsidiaries are simply implementers of the strategies of parent firms. These local implementers have little autonomy to change technology, products, and parts and components. Their task is to sell finished goods.

7 Many American-owned multinational firms prefer top-down management with little delegation of responsibility to local subsidiaries. This lack of autonomy for local subsidiaries is a drag on the firm's ability to perform at the highest levels possible in all global and regional markets in the world.

ECLECTIC PARADIGM

An older view about heterogeneity

Some IB scholars wrote about global strategy as a process of internalization within the firm or internationalization between home and host countries, and they labeled their research results on foreign direct investments with a term from economics, that is, market imperfections. Jean J. Boddewyn of Baruch College of the City University of New York and Thomas Brewer of Georgetown University are just two of many who think in terms of traditional equilibrium analysis rather than the more recent discrete dynamic choice models. Of course, their research occurred before microeconomics made its quantum leap in understanding heterogeneous behavior of nation-states and business firms in the market. As noted in Chapter 6, James Heckman's recent Nobel Lecture on "Micro data, heterogeneity, and the evaluation of public policy" and his other articles underpin a great deal of the recent scholarly work on global strategy. Regretfully, older IB research does not lend itself to discrete dynamic choice modeling now available to newer IB research.

Modifications in IB's eclectic paradigm of international production

John H. Dunning of Reading and Rutgers Universities put together international business's eclectic paradigm of organization, location, and internalization (OLI), and said that all IB phenomena could be incorporated within this paradigm. However, over the past 20 years, external global economic conditions forced Dunning and other academic scholars to modify their views of the eclectic paradigm.

Investment decisions

First, business firms invest overseas, take over foreign firms, and bring them into the parent firm's multinational or multi-local organization. Many of these deals by US, European, and Japanese firms are for the purpose of acquiring foreign-owned technology and markets. The results include changes in organization-specific advantages (O) of subsidiaries in "hot" countries, location-specific advantages (L) in leading-edge industry clusters, and internalization-specific advantages (I) in lowering the cost of doing business internationally.

Market decisions

Second, business firms prefer to stay in rather than exit from markets. Many of their dynamic choices include alliances and partnerships with suppliers, competitors, and buyers in the same and supporting industries; extensive segmentation, targeting, and positioning; and the use of information about the sales and marketing opportunities in emerging countries whose records of economic success are less compelling than Mexico. Modifications in the eclectic paradigm give multinational firms the opportunity to revisit their auto investment strategies *vis-à-vis* Brazil, India, Turkey, and South Africa and Nigeria. The answers to date are YES, YES, NO, NO, and NO.

Managerial decisions

Third, business firms want to control as much as they can through ownership and acquisition, and then through market-based partnerships and alliances. The choices of firms include expanding the boundaries of the firm to include cooperating relationships with subsidiaries owned by other firms. Most of the discussion today on supply channels deals with whether costs and operations are better handled through intra- or inter-firm supplier networks. Japanese auto firms are shifting from intra-firm networks or *keiretsu* to inter-firm supplier networks because costs relationships are changing as Chinese suppliers become more important players in the cooperative relationships among Tier I, Tier II, and Tier III auto and parts firms.

Learning theory

Therefore, IB business executives must teach themselves about nation-state heterogeneity and the important modifications in the eclectic paradigm. These two important additions to their ability to forecast changes in the world economy bring additional order to global strategy. Their host countries will become more diverse over time. Hence, these multinational and multi-local firms will have to prepare diverse country-specific trade and investment strategies. Finally, their suppliers and customers will have to deal with a wider range of heterogeneous choices in incentives, firms, networks, products, and services.

STATE AS STRATEGIST

Case: the Mexican state as strategist

Mexico wooed new investors from established relationships with regional governments in the EU, *keiretsu* links among banks and brother Japanese firms, and party and family links in China and India. Also, Mexico took over competitive positions once held by Canadian provinces and American states. Moreover, Mexico saw earlier than other emerging countries the change coming for FTAs, and it took advantage of this change to cement a new trade and investment relationship with the USA. Finally, Mexico decided to serve most or all of the needs of foreign investors with a tailored set of activities that serve their needs best. In summary, Mexico decided a closer administrative and economic relationship with its more powerful neighbor, the USA, was an appropriate trade-off given the country's ability to maintain the distance between its Iberian-Spanish-Mestizo Catholic culture from the Anglo-American Protestant culture of the USA.

Today, Mexico has a sustainable competitive advantage over all its rival emerging nation-states. Its investment incentives fit together nicely to build up a domestic auto assembly industry that exports cars to the USA. Should other countries within the Americas forge a free trade relationship with the USA (the FTAA will be a major change in structural estimation for Mexico), or should the USA itself enter into free trade with the EU (a North Atlantic FTA will be a major change in treatment effects for Mexico), then Mexico may have to choose a new strategic position, find different trade-offs, and come up with a new fit of activities. Careful attention to public policy strategy offers Mexico the opportunity to maintain its sustainable competitive advantage over its rival emerging countries in Latin America and elsewhere in the world.

A nation-state's strategic capabilities affect the ability of multinational and multi-local firms to manage export and import arrangements, equity joint ventures, and foreign direct investment transactions. Here's what gives countries the operational effectiveness to develop a global-regional strategy.

Local political environment

First, government must have the authority to choose among trade-offs. Second, it must be able to select new investments over the objections of domestic firms. Third, government must impose its sovereign prerogatives to join FTAs. Finally, government must be able to choose among foreign alliances, partners, and investors. These four decisions impose heterogeneity among nation-states. The managerial task for business executives is to delineate the heterogeneous nature of each nation-state, and then develop appropriate corporate global strategies for each and every country within its IB network.

Multinational strategy and structure

Business outcomes of increases in export sales and growth in profits from overseas investments depend on how well IB executives read what is going on within nation-states and how carefully they prepare a corporate business strategy to take advantage of diversity and heterogeneity among countries. This is the paradigm of global strategy.

BUSINESS FIRM AS STRATEGIST

Case: auto industrial clusters within North America

The third attribute of CAGE is geographic nearness or distance between countries as trading partners. When competing and complementary suppliers, firms, and buyers manufacture parts and components, and finished goods in close geographical proximity they are within an industry cluster. Such spatial clustering exists because the geographic region has a pool of specialized workers, inputs from suppliers, managerial knowledge, and rival firms. Multinational firms tap into these leading-edge clusters with their subsidiaries for new ideas, crucial talents, and demanding customers.

Of course, separate geographic clusters within the same industry offer business executives different ways in which to do business. The Canadian auto cluster in Ontario and Quebec is closely tied to the Detroit-based auto cluster. The former exports fully assembled mid-size cars as well as higher value-added parts and components (such as engines and transmissions) for both mid-size and luxury cars. Except for higher levels of labor strife from the Canadian Auto Workers and occasional border-crossing problems of moving cargo from Canada into the USA, the subsidiaries on both sides of the border offer seamless production and distribution to their parent firms and major consumer markets in Toronto, New York, and Chicago. US-owned parent firms dominate the Detroit-Ontario auto cluster and its resident subsidiary firms.

The Mexican auto cluster in northern Mexico fully assembles small cars, lower value-added parts and components (such as brakes, dashboards, gaskets and fasteners) for small and mid-size cars. Except for modest border-crossing problems of moving cargo from Mexico into the USA, the subsidiaries on both sides of the border offer seamless production and distribution to their parent firms and major consumer markets in Los Angeles, Chicago, and Toronto. US- and Japanese-owned parent firms dominate the northern Mexico auto cluster and its resident subsidiary firms.

Owing to the heterogeneous behavior of Mexico, especially in lowering labor and manufacturing costs for new investors, the northern Mexican auto cluster is more dynamic and more responsive to emerging North American market conditions than are the older auto cluster in Ontario and the Canadian government's offers of limited one-off incentives to existing investors. Also, the American owners are the same, and the managerial capabilities of the two sets of subsidiaries are roughly equal. However, the Canadian subsidiaries are so embedded in their local auto cluster because of the 1965 Auto Pact between the two countries that they were careless in dealing with real cultural differences between English-speaking Canadian workers and middle management and their counterparts in the USA.

Finally, with NAFTA in place since 1994, US parent firms made a strategic choice to move some production from Canada and the USA to Mexico. They made a discrete dynamic choice to limit new investment in Ontario and expand foreign direct investment in northern Mexico. Such IB business executive decision making is driven by Mexico's heterogeneous behavior to turn itself into the newest and lowest-cost area of auto production in North America. In this case, the state as strategist won out over traditional business issues of suppliers, decision-making autonomy, sales and marketing, and customers.

Case: transfer of tacit knowledge within auto firms

Organizational-advantage (O) of the eclectic paradigm endorses the idea that the international transfer of technology occurs between a parent firm and its subsidiaries because this type of information is hard to codify or teach to others, or both. The technical term among IB scholars is tacit knowledge.

For example, Ford took control of Mazda and had the latter, its Japanese subsidiary, build a Mazda-type, small-car plant at Hermosillo in northern Mexico. The small cars are exported to the USA and Canada. This is a more efficient internal transfer by Ford than GM's transfer of tacit knowledge to its plant at Ramos Arispe in northern Mexico. Of course, both plants have embedded capabilities because of their location (L) in the northern Mexico auto cluster. They are supported by a wide range of suppliers from whom they buy parts and components through internal intra-firm arrangements or external market transactions or both from locations within Mexico and the USA.

Chrysler's Toluca plant outside Mexico City, VW's plant at Puebla, and Nissan's plant in Aguascalientes are older and contain many factory technologies and management personnel from the pre-NAFTA era. Also, these three plants are far south of the all-important northern Mexico auto cluster. These are a less efficient internal transfer of tacit knowledge. For example, the cars manufactured by Chrysler and VW are for the Mexican market because they lack the styling design and environmental controls demanded by customers and government in the USA. Nissan, similar to other Japanese transplant companies in North America, struggles to keep its supplier network within the internalization (I) of the firm.

Some IB scholars call the process of internalization in the northern Mexico auto cluster an example of successful internal supplier networks and markets, and the process of internalization in central and coastal Mexico an example of failed internal supplier networks and markets. However, the focus of their argument on whether transactions costs are affordable in the market and whether they should be internalized within the firm is misplaced, for the three auto plants are outside the northern Mexico auto cluster.

Instead, VW management in Mexico, which is independent and not integrated with the German parent firm, bought older, out-of-date technology from Germany and never caught up with the demands for newer and better auto technology in the USA. Thus VW management in Germany produced the new models and sold them as nostalgia cars in the USA. Chrysler management in Mexico is a dependent on the US subsidiary and the German parent firm for new technology; its cars stay in Mexico. Nissan management in Mexico sought to reproduce its entire intra-firm supplier, firm, buyer network system in the mountains of central Mexico and failed.

All three firms failed to come up with a cost-effective process of internalization and all three had transactional difficulties in the market. Also, they could not train personnel fast enough to reduce the opportunities for internal and market failure. Moreover, these three auto investors failed in their quest for ownership-specific (O) advantages. Thus they could not demonstrate the relative efficiency of internal transfer versus market transfer within the Mexican auto market. Let's conclude with the idea that these three firms were less successful in transferring tacit knowledge between the parent firm and subsidiaries than were Ford and Mazda in Mexico.

Heterogeneity of pre- and post-NAFTA Mexico

Before NAFTA, the Mexican state as strategist insisted that auto manufacturers produce 75 percent of their cars within Mexico. This is the national content rule. Model runs in plants were short and costs were high. Additional models at lower costs were smuggled into Mexico from the USA. After NAFTA, the Mexican state as strategist called on auto manufacturers to integrate their Mexican and US operations. Business firms as strategist took over to introduce the tacit knowledge of the parent firm into their Mexican subsidiaries. Ford was the most successful with its completely new plant. GM came in second with its redesigned plant. And the others with their older factories fell way behind the front-runners.

Bruce Kogut of the University of Pennsylvania and Udo Zander of the Stockholm School of Economics make the following point: "Firms tend to do what they have done before ... They accumulate and communicate social knowledge ... This tacit knowledge is not easily bought and sold in markets ... Instead, firms invest in new organizations (O), locations (L), and new technologies (I) to take advantage of new market opportunities."

In summary, Ford's management was the first to see the opportunity of Mexico in NAFTA. It was so fast off the mark that it gained first-mover advantage in the race to be the most important firm that manufactures cars in Mexico for sale throughout North America. Ford's global-regional strategy is about two crucial ideas: Emerging countries such as Mexico present a different set of heterogeneous characteristics in the pre- and post-FTA markets; and business firms such as Ford must develop global-regional strategies based on these pre- and post FTA differences.

Case: strategy and structure in a local Indian auto subsidiary

Unless the local subsidiary has the world mandate to produce one item at the lowest cost possible, such as pressurized caps for radiators or flanged fasteners for securing motors to the engine blocks, overseas auto subsidiaries are local implementers of the decisions by parent firms. According to Julian M. Birkinshaw of the Stockholm School of Economics and Allen J. Morrison of the American Graduate School of

International Management (Thunderbird), the global-regional strategy of parent firms and local implementing subsidiaries is as follows:

» Emerging countries such as India pressure both parents and local subsidiaries for national responsiveness.
» Business firms such as Ford offer their local implementing subsidiaries low strategic autonomy, high product dependence on the parent, low international configuration of manufacturing, and low international configuration of downstream activities.

Ford's plant in Madras (Chennai), India has limited geographic scope. It manufactures cars for India only. Also, it first produced a car in India that was ten years out of date when it was introduced in India; the car never caught on. In the late 1990s, Ford introduced the Ikon car. It was designed for the Indian market. It had more headroom for those who wear turbans; it had more legroom and separate air conditioning in the back for the owner-passenger; it had modern styling. Still the Ikon was a severely constrained product with little value-added to commend itself to Indian consumers. Ford's Indian plant is closely integrated with the parent firm and the former has limited managerial and engineering responsibilities. The Madras plant purchases parts and components from other subsidiaries and the parent firm itself within the Ford family. In short, the local plant sells and markets its auto product in the local Indian market.

Unfortunately for Ford, the Ikon car has not gained popular acceptance among Indian consumers. A J.D. Powers study found that Indian customers did not see the Ikon as uniquely different from other cars manufactured and sold in India. Ford in India is not a good example of the fit between strategy and structure that must happen to make subsidiaries successful overseas.

Case: auto firms in Europe and the USA as multicontract organizations

Parent auto firms have both explicit and implicit contracts that link the parent firm with its subsidiaries, tie the subsidiaries together, and do deals with supplier and buyer networks. All players have incentives to engage in contracts – for example, between Ford's American and European operations in which successful managers are transferred back and forth across the North Atlantic to shore up weaknesses in the USA or Germany. Although implicit understandings are paramount in these managerial exchanges, not all contingencies are foreseen or revealed to top management.

Here are some questions about performance. Will European families be happy in Dearborn, Michigan, USA? Will American teenagers want to live within a more traditional society? Will American managers be able to deal with European labor unions, banks, and other stakeholders in German and UK plants? Can European managers handle a continental distribution system with supplier links into Canada and Mexico?

The problem for managers is that heterogeneous stakeholders will answers these questions with different answers. A few European-owned global firms, such as Nestlé, favor independent US subsidiaries. A few American-owned multinational firms, such as Gillette, put in place a North Atlantic product/market group as a way to minimize the number of different answers. Most American-owned multinational firms, such as Ford, insist that successful European-based executives be transferred to the USA to help rebuild the American parent firm. This heavy-handiness depletes the European operations of the firm just when such managerial talent is needed.

Thus Europe might engage in hidden gaming, or exchanges that are not under the control of the parent firm. Here the history of the organization becomes important. Although both Ford and GM maintain a bureaucracy that is typical in size and scope for large firms, Ford runs its business top down while GM prefers horizontal relationships. Ford would not be fertile ground for teams across the North Atlantic, but it would be fertile ground for hidden gaming. Since Ford has no explicit contracts between its European and American operations, few of the individual successes in either locale will be recognized by the parent firm. Without recognition, no amount of incentives will change the relationship between the parent firm and its subsidiaries.

Summary of Ford's successes and failures

Here is a testable hypothesis: Ford might have done better in terms of successful market entry and penetration by offering a more top-down approach to management control. The cases discussed above belie this statement. Let's draw the following conclusions:

» Ford in Mexico as a part of NAFTA is a great success. The subsidiary has autonomy to manufacture small cars and sell them in the USA.
» Ford in India is not a great success because it simply implements the product strategy of the parent firm. Ford in India lacks autonomy.
» Ford between the USA and Europe suffers from Ford's insistence on a top-down organization.

Forecast

Nation-states offer multinational firms two sets of heterogeneous behavior pre- and post-FTAs. Parent firms that give their local subsidiaries autonomy to make decisions on technology, managerial competence, and sales and marketing opportunities. Those parent firms that do not give their local subsidiaries autonomy do less well overseas. Hence, Ford always will be in second place after GM in the race for dominance in the world's auto industry.

SOURCES

Julian Birkinshaw and Neil Hood, "Characteristics of foreign subsidiaries in industry clusters," *Journal of International Business Studies*, 31:1 (First Quarter 2000): 141-154.

Julian Birkinshaw and Allen J. Morrison, "Configuration of strategy and structure in subsidiaries of multinational corporations," *Journal of International Business Studies*, 26:4 (Fourth Quarter 1995): 729-753.

Jean J. Boddewyn, "Political aspects of MNE theory," *Journal of International Business Studies*, 19:3 (Fall 1998): 341-364.

Thomas L. Brewer, "Government policies, market imperfections, and foreign direct investment," *Journal of International Business Studies*, 24:1 (First Quarter 1993): 101-120.

John H. Dunning, "Reappraising the eclectic paradigm in an age of alliance capitalism," *Journal of International Business Studies*, 26:3 (Third Quarter 1995): 461-492.

Bruce Kogut and Udo Zander, "Knowledge, market failure, and the multinational enterprise: a reply," *Journal of International Business Studies*, 46:2 (Second Quarter 1995): 417-426.

Jean-Jacques Laffont and David Martimont, "The firm as a multicontract organization," *Journal of Economics and Management Strategy*, 6:2 (Summer 1997): 201–234.

Stefanie Ann Lenway and Thomas P. Murtha, "The state as strategist in international business research," *Journal of International Business Studies*, 25:3 (Third Quarter 1994): 513–536.

James H. Love, "Knowledge, market failure and the multinational enterprise: a theoretical note," *Journal of International Business Studies*, 26:2 (Second Quarter 1995): 399–408.

Michael E. Porter, "What is strategy?" *Harvard Business Review*, 74:6 (November–December 1996): 61–78.

Key Concepts and Thinkers

» Approximately 1,500-word entries on major related concepts and thinkers.

Global strategy contributes the following to the world economy:

» It offers the opportunity for national success through free trade areas. FTAs do the following: reduce country risk; show how entry strategies work well under different national norms; offer world-class, standardized products, but use locally produced goods when national culture requires a modification in the product mix; provide a venue for global brands to be sold worldwide. Example: Global-regional discount retail strategy of Wal-Mart within NAFTA.

» It shapes (and is shaped by) management, organizational, market, and public strategy. Examples: Ryanair and EasyJet find the boundaries set by nation-states. Arm, JCB, and others look for low-cost opportunities that keep European firms competitive with US firms. Tesco ties bricks-and-mortar and online retailing together.

» It looks for sales and marketing opportunities in "hot" countries. Examples: Developed countries are the USA, Canada, Germany, France, Finland, Italy, Japan. Emerging countries are Mexico, Korea, mainland China, Singapore, Brazil, Bangalore (India), and Turkey. Look for heterogeneous variations in national socio-cultural characteristics.

» It compares transaction costs between intra- and inter-firm supplier, firm, and buyer networks. It asks these questions: What are the switching costs? What are the real boundaries of the firm? How to form cooperative alliances? What can be accomplished through e-commerce? Examples: *Keiretsu*, Japanese auto supplier networks, and mainland Chinese computer chip buyer groups.

» It builds up nations and regions as brands, and creates a new set of celebrities among emerging countries lucky to be within FTAs. Examples: northern Mexico within NAFTA; and the west of Ireland, the south of Spain, Reggio Emilia of northern Italy, the *Mezzogiorno* of southern Italy, and the eastern region of Germany within the EU.

» It prefers cultural and administrative similarities, geographic nearness, and similar levels of economic success, or the CAGE methodology. Examples: Canada and the USA are siblings. The UK and the USA are first cousins. Mexico and the USA are second cousins. The USA has 15 friends in the EU. Both the US and EU are strangers in East and South Asia.

» It fosters both nation-states and firms as strategists, and puts them together in industrial clusters in which to make investment, market, and managerial decisions. Examples: Transfer of tacit knowledge within the auto industrial clusters of northern Mexico and western Ontario-Detroit, Michigan.

» It brings together international business, country risk, and economics and management strategy into short- mid-, and long-term successes. The ten steps are:
  » Dominate FTAs.
  » Select "hot" countries.
  » Marry old and new economy.
  » Create new infrastructure.
  » Teach regions new competitive behaviors.
  » Calculate costs of value-added services. Provide distinctive products in mature markets.
  » Confront network effects.
  » Be a smart mover.
  » Prepare for the future.
  » Check out the new rules for alliances, partnerships, and nonequity joint ventures between Russian and American firms.

All the following key concepts and thinkers enrich the discussion on global strategy.

Acquisitions – Purchase of existing plant and equipment.

Alliances – Nonequity arrangements for the common use of supplier and buyer networks.

Andean Pact – Free trade agreement among the Andean countries of South America: Venezuela, Colombia, Ecuador, Peru, Bolivia.

Asean – Free trade agreement among the South East Asian and Indo-china countries: Thailand, Malaysia, Singapore, The Philippines, Indonesia, Brunei, Myanmar (Burma), Vietnam, Cambodia, Laos.

Asia-Pacific Economic Consensus Group or APEC – Free trade discussions among the Asian, and North and South American countries bordering on the Pacific Ocean.

Backward induction – Weigh sovereign risk of government bonds, foreign exchange value of national currencies, investment climates for sales and profits, and the brand viability of nation-states.

Bartlett, Christopher A. and Sumantra Ghosal – *Managing Across Borders: The Transnational Solution*.

Besanko, David – *The Economics of Strategy*.

Big emerging markets or BEMs – Chinese commonwealth of mainland China, Hong Kong, and Taiwan; India; South Korea; Mexico; Brazil; Argentina; South Africa; Poland; Turkey; Asean countries.

Brand capital – Build up the brand name and its recognition among customers so it is a valuable asset separate from the product itself.

Brand image – Emerging countries within FTAs as celebrities.

CAGE – Culture, administration, geography, and economics.

Clusters – A group of firms in the same industry and usually within the same region or geographic space.

Contractor, Farok. J., and Peter Lorange – *Cooperative Strategies in International Business*.

Copyrights – Intellectual property. TRIPS. Protects original works. Berne Convention.

Corporate culture – Attitudes, habits, and practices of managers within firms.

Country risk – Political, economic, cultural, business, and financial risks.

Cultural distance – Differences among nation-states about habits, values, and customs.

Cyinkota, Michael R. and Ilkka A. Ronkainen, eds – *Best Practices in International Business*.

Developed economies – Industrialized countries with high levels of disposable personal income.

Diffusion – Country effect and time effect on the adoption of new products.

Discount retail culture – Innovations in merchandising, logistics, and information technology at the lowest possible price.

Dunning, John – *Economic Analysis and the Multinational Enterprise. The Globalization of Business: The Challenge of the 1990s*.

Eclectic paradigm – Organization, location, and internalization or OLI.

E-commerce – Electronic business between firms and with customers.

Economic development – Stages of economic growth of countries.

Emerging countries – Partially industrialized countries with lower levels of disposable personal income.

Entry decisions – Go into a host country as a first mover.

European Union or EU – Customs union of 15 European countries: France, Germany, Italy, The Netherlands, Belgium, Luxembourg, United Kingdom, Ireland, Denmark, Greece, Spain, Portugal, Austria, Sweden, Finland.

Experience goods – Exports and foreign direct investments.

First-mover advantage – The first company to sell goods and gain substantial market share over their competitors.

Foreign direct investment or FDI – Direct investment overseas.

Free trade agreements or FTAs – Two or more countries reduce or eliminate or both tariffs on goods among themselves. Sometimes, these nation-states also reduce or eliminate the restrictions on services, and capital and labor mobility.

Free Trade Agreement of the Americas or FTAA – A proposed agreement to reduce or eliminate (or both) tariffs on goods among all countries (except Cuba) in the western hemisphere.

Friedman, Thomas – *The Lexus and the Olive Tree: Understanding Globalization.*

Geographic nearness and distance – Nation-states are either close or far away.

Globalization – 1980s to the present in which products and services, and customers, are more similar today than they were 40 years ago.

Global strategy – Comprehensive effort by firms to manufacture and sell products worldwide.

Global-regional strategy – Comprehensive effort by firms to manufacture and sell products within an FTA.

Greenfield investments – Completely new investments in plant and equipment.

Gross domestic product or GDP – The domestic output of a nation.

Group of Seven or G7 – Group of seven industrial nations: United States, Japan, Germany, United Kingdom, France, Italy, Canada.

Heterogeneous countries – Nation-states present different socio-economic characteristics to business firms.

Home country – Country in which the parent firm is based.

Host country – Country in which the parent firm is allowed to do business under local laws.

Hot countries – Nation-states with good sales and marketing opportunities.

Intellectual property – Patents, trademarks, copyrights.

International diversification – Sell products and investing in overseas markets.

James, Harold – *The End of Globalization: Lessons from the Great Depression.*

Joint ventures – 50–50 percent equity partnerships (equity joint ventures), or nonequity cooperative alliances (nonequity joint ventures).

Journals – American Economic Review. California Management Review. Daedalus. Harvard Business Review. Journal of Economics and Management Strategy. Journal of International Business Studies. Journal of Political Economy. Sloan Management Review. Strategic Management Review.

Just-in-time inventory or JIT – Ideal for a manufacturing plant is to keep no inventory. Practical for a factory is to keep a minimum level of inventory.

Keiretsu – Japanese business organization centered around a bank with a group of cooperating firms from many industries. They all have equity shares in each other's businesses and share boards of directors.

Lamont, Douglas – *Conquering the Wireless World: The Age of M-Commerce. Global Marketing. Salmon Day: the End of the Beginning for Global Business. Winning Worldwide: Strategies for Dominating Global Business.*

Learning theory – Suppliers, firms, buyers, and customers teach themselves about new products and services.

Management strategy – Set of strategic actions and objectives.

Market strategy – Set of 4 Ps (product, price, promotion, place) marketing strategies.

Mercosur – Free trade agreement for southern South America. Brazil, Argentina, Paraguay, Uruguay.

Multicontract organizations – contracts between parent firms and subsidiaries, among subsidiaries, and with supplier networks.

Multi-local firms – Committed to and reflects home country.

Multinational firms – Emotional connection to home country.

National culture – Socio-cultural characteristics of nation-states.

Nation-states – Politically independent countries.

Newspapers – *Financial Times. The New York Times. The Wall Street Journal.*

North American Free Trade Agreement or NAFTA – Free trade for three North American countries, Canada, United States, Mexico.

Offshore assembly – Manufacture of goods outside home country.

Ohmae, Kenichi – *The Borderless World. The End of the Nation State: The Rise of Regional Economies. Triad Power.*

Organization for Economic and Community Development or OECD – Groups of industrial and newly industrialized nations.

Organizational strategy – Buy or build plants, or outsource manufacturing.

Original equipment manufacturers or OEMs – Producers of brand-named parts and components.

Partnerships – Alliances or nonequity joint ventures or both.

Patent – Intellectual property. TRIPS. First-to-file vs. first-to-invent (only the USA and The Philippines).

Porter, Michael E. – *Competitive Strategy. Competitive Analysis. Competitive Analysis of Nations.*

Prahalad, C.K. and Yves L. Doz – *The Multinational Mission: Balancing Local Demands and Global Vision.*

Public strategy – Legal and social restraints on foreign trade and foreign direct investments.

Rangan, Subramanian and Robert Z. Lawrence – *A Prism on Globalization.*

Robinson, Richard D. – *Direct Foreign Investment: Costs and Benefits.*

Rostow, W.W. – *The Stages of Economic Growth.*

Rugman, Alan – *New Theories of the Multinational Enterprise.*

Strategic alliances – Partnerships and nonequity joint ventures.

Switching costs – The costs of moving from one country to another, and changing supplier, firm, buyer networks.

Tacit knowledge – Technology, intellectual property, and management competence embedded in products.

Toyne, Brian and Douglas Nigh - *International Business: An Emerging Vision.*

Trademarks - Brand names. Intellectual property. TRIPS. Paris Convention.

Trade-related intellectual property rights or TRIPS - Patents, trademarks, copyrights.

Transaction costs - The cost to buy goods or services or both in markets.

Value chain - Accumulation of value and increasing margin through the primary activities of sourcing, logistics, manufacturing, marketing, and service.

Vernon, Ray - *Sovereignty at Bay.*

World Trade Organization or WTO - Nation-states join together to regularize trade rules and settle disputes.

Yip, George S. - *Total Global Strategy.*

This list shows the richness of global strategy.

Resources[1]

» Easy reference to everything covered in the book.
» Suggestions for further reading.
» Useful Websites.

Here is a library of important sources for implementing a global strategy:

» Seminal articles give details about important themes.
» Thoughtful books share the big picture.
» Useful Websites help practitioners and researchers find the latest information.

At the end are recent articles. They have not been judged as seminal by practitioners and researchers, but they help shape how marketers carry out their global strategy in today's world economy.

SEMINAL ARTICLES

» Comparison of US and Japanese strategies. J.K. Johansson and George S. Yip, "Exploiting globalization potential: U.S. and Japanese strategies," *Strategic Management Journal* (October 1994): 579-601.
» Core competency. C.K. Prahalad and Gary Hamel, "The core competence of the corporation," *Harvard Business Review,* 68 (May-June 1990): 70-91.
» Effective decision making faced with differing levels of uncertainty. Hugh Courtney et al., "Strategy under uncertainty," *Harvard Business Review* (November-December 1997): 66-79.
» Fluid organizational structures for equity and nonequity arrangements in global markets. Bruce Kogut, "Designing global strategies: profiting from operational flexibility," *Sloan Management Review,* 27 (1985): 27-38.
» Industry clusters. Michael E. Porter, "Competition, and economic development: local clusters in a global economy," *Economic Development Quarterly,* 14:1 (February 2000): 15-34.
» Interfirm alliances are not based solely on transaction costs. Ranjay Gulati, "Does familiarity breed trust? The implications of repeated ties for contractual choice in alliances," *Academy of Management Journal,* 38 (February 1995): 85-112.
» Limits to globalization. Dani Rodrik, "Has globalization gone too far," *California Management Review,* 39:3 (Spring 1997): 29-53.
» Revision of traditional organizational model. William G. Egelhoff, "Strategy and structure in multinational corporations: a revision of the Stopford and Wells Model," *Strategic Management Journal,* 9:1 (January-February 1988): 1-14.

» Role of strategy during periods of expansion. Denis Rondinelli *et al.*, "The struggle for strategic alignment in multinational corporations: managing readjustments during global expansion," *European Management Journal*, 194 (August 2001): 404–416.

» Strategy deals with unique activities that ideally cannot be imitated by competitors. Components of a strategic product and service mix can complement one another, thus enhancing operational efficiencies. Michael E. Porter, "What is strategy?" *Harvard Business Review* (November–December 1996): 61–89.

» Strategy defined as looking beyond present-day problems towards future opportunities. Gary Hamel and C.K. Prahalad, "Strategic intent," *Harvard Business Review* (May–June 1989): 63–76.

» Tools multinationals use to achieve their strategy objectives. Sumantra Ghoshal, "Global strategy: an organizing framework," *Strategic Management Journal*, 8: 5 (September–October 1987): 425–440.

» US corporate response to Japanese competition in the mid-1980s. C.K. Prahalad and Gary Hamel, "Do you really have a strategy," *Harvard Business Review* (July–August 1985): 139–148.

THOUGHTFUL BOOKS

» Application of microeconomics to management and strategy. David Besanko *et al.*, *The Economics of Strategy* (New York: John Wiley & Sons, 1996).

» Articles about global strategy. *Global Strategies: Insights from the World's Leading Thinkers* (Cambridge, Mass.: Harvard Business Review Book, 1994).

» Challenges of globalization in the 1990s. John H. Dunning, *The globalization of business: The challenge of the 1990s* (London: Routledge, 1993).

» Corporate responses. Subramanian Rangan and Robert Z. Lawrence, *A Prism on Globalization* (Washington, DC: Brookings Institution Press, 1999).

» Culture's influence on global business strategy. David Landes, *The Wealth and Poverty of Nations: Why Some Are So Rich and Others Are So Poor* (New York: W.W. Norton, 1998).

» Examining knowledge as an intangible asset. Karl Erik Sveiby, *The New Organizational Wealth: Managing and Measuring Knowledge-Based Assets* (San Francisco: Berrett-Koehler, 1997).
» Global strategy of multinational firms. George Yip, *Total Global Strategy* (Englewood Cliffs, NJ: Prentice Hall, 1992).
» Industrial clusters and nation-states. Michael E. Porter, *The Competitive Advantage of Nations* (New York: The Free Press, 1990).
» Nonequity arrangements. Farok J. Contractor and Peter Lorange, *Cooperative Strategies in International Business* (Lexington, Mass.: Lexington Books, 1998).
» Organizational structure of American multinationals. John M. Stopford and Louis T. Wells, *Managing the Multinational Enterprise: Organization of the Firm and Ownership of the Subsidiaries* (New York: Basic Books, 1972).
» Problems inherent in global business. Christopher A. Bartlett and Sumantra Goshal, *Managing Across Borders: The Transnational Solution* (Boston: Harvard Business School Press, 1998).
» Return of nation-states in controlling multinational firms. Douglas Lamont, *Salmon Day: The End of the Beginning for Global Business* (Oxford, UK: Capstone Publishers Ltd., 1997).
» Suggests the end of national barriers to global business. Kenichi Ohmae, *The Borderless World*, (London: Collins, 1990).
» Think global, act local is the theme. C.K. Prahalad and Yves L. Doz, *The Multinational Mission: Balancing Local Demands and Global Vision* (New York: Free Press, 1987).

USEFUL WEBSITES

» Access to the EU institutions and descriptions of their activities. European Union (EU) Online. http://europa.eu.int
» Access to Internet-based information on country background, economic development and international trade. Latin American Network Information Center (LANIC). http://www.lanic.utexas.edu
» Access to leading business magazines and top national newspapers, including *Wall Street Journal*, Dow Jones & Reuters newswires,

market research reports, and analyst reports. Dow Jones Interactive. http://askdj.dowjones.com

» Aimed at professional buyers who deal directly with manufacturers, agents or distributors. Kompass. http://www.kompass.com

» Bilingual site permitting sourcing agents to locate, contact, and buy from suppliers online. Latin Supplier. http://www.latinsupplier.com

» Contains 30 member countries sharing a commitment to democratic government and the market economy. Its work covers economic and social issues from macroeconomics, to trade, education, development. Organization for Economic Co-operation and Development (OECD). http://www.oecd.org.

» Covers suppliers in ten European countries. Who Supplies What? http://web.wlwonline.de

» Current awareness service with daily updates on economic and financial news in 200 countries; with full text. Investing, Licensing and Training. EIU.com. http://www.EIU.com

» Database contains content from thousands of journals that help researchers track business conditions, trends, management techniques, corporate strategies, and industry-specific topics worldwide. ABI/Inform. http://www.umi.com/proquest

» Directory of manufacturers and distributors from 17 European countries. Thomas Register – Europe. http://www.tipcoeurope.com

» Founded as MeetChina.com, this service now encompasses other Asian nations and provides an interface for purchasers and suppliers. Meet World Trade. http://www.meetworldtrade.com

» Includes US import/export data, international market research reports, and the text of Basic Guide to Exporting. StatUSA. http://www.stat-usa.gov

» Information source for the procurement, supply-chain and management professional in the electronics industry. Electronic Buyers News. http://www.ebnonline.com

» Leading publication containing trade and shipping news. Journal of Commerce. http://www.joc.com

» Links arranged by region or individual nation-states. Virtual International Business and Economic Sources (VIBES). http://libweb.uncc. edu/ref-bus/vibehome.htm

» Multi-industry business database with a strong global focus on company, product and industry information providing facts, figures and trends needed for gaining a strategic and competitive edge. Business and Industry. http://www.galegroup.com/welcome.html
» Official site of only global international organization dealing with the rules of trade between nations. World Trade Organization (WTO). http://www.wto.org
» Official site the world's largest free trade zone. Free Trade Area of the Americas. http://www.ftaa-alca.org
» Portal offers connections to international business professionals worldwide. GlobalEdge. http://www.globaledge.msu.edu
» Product and trade information for volume buyers. Global Sources. http://www.globalsources.com
» Promotes trade and investment with Japan. Japan External Trade Organization (JETRO). http://www.jetro.go.jp
» Through its resources and a network of 180 affiliated organizations, NAPM provides opportunities for expansion of professional skills and knowledge. National Association of Purchasing Managers. http://www.NAPM.org
» US Customs site with links to Canadian and Mexican counterparts. NAFTA. http://www.nafta-customs.org

RECENT PUBLICATIONS

» Costs of supplier networks. Stephen Roach, "Back to borders," *Financial Times*, September 28, 2001, p. 14.
» Discusses the possibility of the world swinging away from globalization. Harold James, *The End of Globalization: Lessons from the Great Depression* (Cambridge, Mass.: Harvard University Press, 2001).
» Explains a theory of global collapse. Thomas D. Jeitschko and Curtis R. Taylor, "Local discouragement and global collapse: a theory of coordination avalanches, *American Economic Review*, 91:1 (March 2001): 208-224.
» Spells out the critiques of globalization. 'Globalisation and its critics,' *The Economist*, September 29, 2001, pp. Survey 3-30.
Read these materials to get a more complete picture of global strategy.

NOTE

1 This chapter was written with the assistance of Brian DeHart, Research Librarian, DePaul University.

Ten Steps to Making Global Strategy Work

- » Distilled wisdom of case studies.
- » Practical advice on how to make global strategy work, and how to have realistic expectations of what you can expect from global strategy.

Global strategy is a product of several interrelated fields of study about managerial decision making within the world economy. These are as follows: international business, country risk, and economics and management strategy. By combining these three concepts, business executives grow export sales and invest in overseas markets, pay attention to free trade among developed countries and with emerging countries, and prosper by matching their products and services to the differences inherent in heterogeneous nation-states. In short, global strategy puts all of these ideas together and then sorts them out in new ways so business executives can prepare for the future.

SHORT-TERM SUCCESS

The short-term success of business executives depends on choices among *international business* strategies. These are outlined by the eclectic paradigm, or OLI (organization, location, and internalization):

» **Entry**: Exports, alliances, partnerships, nonequity joint ventures, equity joint ventures, acquisitions of locally owned firms, "greenfield" or new investments in plant and equipment. Focus is on foreign trade or direct investment by firms, and how OLI helps explain decisions to enter new markets.

» **Operations**: Costs of and benefits from intra- and inter-firm supplier, firm, and buyer networks; Four Ps (product, price, promotion, place) marketing strategies; foreign exchange; global, multinational, multilocal, and domestic business firms. Focus is on internal managerial decisions within firms, and how OLI helps explain the boundaries of firms within networks.

MID-TERM SUCCESS

The mid-term success of business executives depends on an expanded view of *country risk*. It is outlined by one variable of the eclectic paradigm, or location (L) of OLI, and other ideas from trade law, demography, sociology, and values and lifestyles:

» **Regional free trade**: NAFTA, EU, APEC, and others. Focus is on improving the collective economic performance of countries within FTAs through global-regional strategies of business firms.

» **Levels of economic development**: Developed and emerging countries. Focus is on improving the ability of emerging countries to compete against developed countries through new foreign direct investments by supplier, firm, buyer networks.
» **National culture**: Demographics, socio-economic characteristics, history, language, values and lifestyles. Focus is on promoting countries and regions as brand names worthy of international celebrity.

LONG-TERM SUCCESS

The long-term success of business executives depends on applied theories from *economics and management strategy*. They are hinted at by the eclectic paradigm or OLI (organization, location, and internalization). However, they are more carefully spelled out by the availability of microeconomic data, a review of transaction costs, and decisions about how to embed tacit knowledge within business firms:

» **Nation-states as heterogeneous agents**: Some are "hot" countries and others do not have good sales and marketing opportunities. Focus is on how nation-states and their regions convey investment and market possibilities to foreign firms, and what will it cost these firms to switch from one industrial cluster or location to another.
» **Business firms as multicontract organizations**: Some firms have both equity and nonequity deals, and these could be with private or state-owned enterprises, with national labor organizations, or other stakeholders. Focus is on how business firms deal with nation-states, local partners, and other market players to grow sales and earn profits.

TEN STEPS TO MAKING GLOBAL STRATEGY WORK

Here are the ten steps towards global strategy success:

1 Dominate regional free trade markets.
2 Select "hot" countries.
3 Marry old and new economy.
4 Create new infrastructure.
5 Teach regions new competitive behaviors.

6 Calculate costs of value-added services.
7 Provide distinctive and exclusive products in mature markets.
8 Confront network effects.
9 Be a smart mover.
10 Prepare for the future.

These steps are illustrated in the following case studies.

Wal-Mart dominates NAFTA market

Step one is for firms to dominate their home market first, grow the business in neighboring free trade markets, and make entry choices in far-away overseas markets. After the USA, Wal-Mart took its retail merchandising business to Canada and Mexico and made it a success in both NAFTA countries. Wal-Mart did less well elsewhere in the world. In Argentina and Germany, local national cultures dominate Wal-Mart's managerial decisions to introduce North American-style retail merchandising in Latin America and western Europe.

In summary, Wal-Mart made good choices about its international business investments in Canada and Mexico. These are highly successful because the firm's analysis of country risk was superior to other US-owned discount retailers. Wal-Mart correctly saw the heterogeneity among the nations of North America. The firm selected its merchandise, arranged the internal layout of its store, and chose its urban locations to reflect the different national characters of the USA, Canada, and Mexico. Wal-Mart's ability to deliver an excellent retail product stopped customers from switching to other discount retailers. Therefore, Wal-Mart's global-regional strategy is a great success within NAFTA.

Vodafone and Deutsche Telekom select "hot" countries

Both UK-owned Vodafone and German-owned Deutsche Telekom provide cellular telephone service through the wireless application protocol (WAP) of the European-wide GSM system. Vodafone came first to the USA. It bought Pacific Bell's wireless service and converted the latter to GSM. Later it became a partner in Verizon's code division multiple access (CDMA) protocol. Only in 2001 did Deutsche Telekom acquire VoiceStream Wireless and its GSM protocol. Both European firms bet that the USA would move quickly into wireless telephony. They were wrong, because the USA still lacks a general consensus on how fast to overcome its technology diffusion problems. Moreover, although GSM has wide appeal in Europe, Asia, and other parts of the world, the US GSM "footprint" of these two European firms pales in comparison to CDMA and other wireless protocols in the USA. Their initial foreign direct investments were not sufficient to convert the USA to a new wireless technology.

In summary, these two European providers of GSM made less than sterling choices in foreign direct investments in the USA. They failed to correctly assess the country risk of the country, especially in how long it would take the US federal government to make decisions about moving from analogue to digital telephone service, and then from 2G to 3G digital wireless telephones. Both Vodafone and DT failed to pay attention to the USA as a heterogeneous agent with real differences that could slam down foreign-owned firms. Hence, their American customers could and did switch to CDMA providers once the one- or two-year contracts were completed. Therefore, the global-regional strategy of Vodafone and Deutsche Telekom is not a success in the USA.

Z.R.E. Grodeck marries old and new economy

Poland's Z.R.E. Grodeck forges, bangs, and welds pieces of metal into boilers, racks, pumps, and other parts for heavy industry at Swiecie, about a three-and-a-half-hour drive northwest of Warsaw. It uses a personal computer to dial up a business-to-business website in the USA, sells product electronically to central and eastern Europe, and bids on contracts for American manufacturers who seek cheaper sources for labor-intensive products. For example, Z.R.E. builds hundreds of metal frames for moving sheets of glass around a factory; these are used in the American plants of Pilkington, a British glass maker. Z.R.E. has adapted its traditional business to the Internet. In 1999, the Polish firm was acquired by US-owned Universal Process Equipment.

In summary, the American parent firm made a good investment in Poland. It assessed its country risk and saw to it that its Polish subsidiary had telephone access to the Internet. Since Poland is not yet within the European Union, it displays even more differences in economic development than its western European neighbors, especially as a former communist country that aspires to be an equal to Germany and others in the EU. Therefore, the regional-local strategy of Universal Process Equipment and its Z.R.E. subsidiary is a success.

American firms create new infrastructure in Japan

Here are a few examples. L.L. Bean, Eddie Bauer Inc., and Lands' End began their entry into Japan through catalog mailings. Through Internet sales at kiosks in *konbini* and in local retail stores they are firmly entrenched in Japan. American International Group (AIG) now sells directly to Japanese consumers. McDonald's has over 2,000 outlets in Japan. Morgan Stanley Dean Witter & Co. opened retail financial branches in Japan. Seven-Eleven offers the Japanese world-class efficiency and profitability.

Japan presents several major market impediments. These are as follows:

1 Japanese business practices such as cultural barriers and *keiretsu* or close business linkages;
2 Japanese expectations of excessive high quality and unreasonable high standards, inadequate import infrastructure, and delays in patent and trademark processing;
3 high cost of doing business in Japan, such as a lack of economies of scale, high entry cost, and high retail prices;
4 preference for Japan-made products and an unwillingness to purchase foreign products.

American firms that improved foreign penetration of the Japanese market did the following: adapted products to suit local cultural norms, carried out more service, collaborated with local firms, had a long-term orientation, trained personnel better, and responded quicker to complaints.

In summary, some American firms made good investments in Japan. They assessed cultural risk and did what was necessary to make changes in products and services so that their goods became less foreign and more Japanese to local customers. Although Japan has been in a decade-long deep recession, the global-regional retail and distribution strategies of these American firms are a great success.

Brand-name regions learn new competitive behaviors

These are rank-ordered within their geographic region. Each region is an industrial cluster:

» Americas:
  » Northern Mexico, western Ontario, Canada and their contiguous areas in the US. Auto industry;
  » Southern and southeastern Brazil, and contiguous areas in Argentina and Uruguay. Autos and farm equipment.
» Europe:
  » Southern England, Scottish lowlands, and southwestern Ireland. China dishes.
  » Benelux countries of Belgium, the Netherlands, and Luxembourg. Packaging and import redistribution.
  » Fos (Marseilles), Catalonia (Spain), Reggio Emilia (Italy), Dresden and Leipzig (southeastern Germany), Poland-A (next to eastern Germany), Prague (Czech Republic), Budapest (Hungary), and Moscow region (Russia). Mixed heavy and light industries.
» East and South Asia:
  » Southern and coastal China from Shanghai to Hong Kong, and Manchuria. Electronics and auto industries.
  » Taiwan, Singapore, high-tech corridor of Malaysia, and eastern shore region of Thailand. Electronics and computer industries.
  » Tokyo and Osaka regions of Japan. Photo electric sensors, autos, telephones, and many other light and heavy industries.
  » Bangalore and Hyderabad city-regions of India. Information technology and call back telephone services.
» Other regions:
  » Israel–Palestine–Jordan. Software and computer industries.
  » South Africa. Mixed heavy and light industries.

Each region and industrial cluster has its own country risk story. National culture and character are crucial elements in decisions to invest in or exit from a region. Some are developed regions and within successful FTAs; more are emerging industrial centers and usually outside FTAs. International business decisions about entry and operations play a more important role in decision making than do more sophisticated attempts at microeconomic analysis. Many of these regions are part of supplier, firm, buyer networks that are within global, multinational, and multi-local firms. Others simply sell commodities, parts and components, and in-process goods to business firms. The most successful regions were discussed in this and other chapters of the book.

Shanghai's Linktone provides value-added mobile phone services

Most Chinese have not had much exposure to PCs, so mobile phones have provided their first, high-tech interface with short messaging services (SMS), the Web and the Internet. China's mobile phone users are double the population of the UK (60 million) and nearing the population of the USA (270 million). China's mobile phone users use their mobile handsets to adopt and care for virtual "pets," such as tigers, pigs, and koalas, similar to the Japanese electronic pet, *Tamagotchi*. China's pet park is run by Linktone, the Shanghai-based value-added mobile data service provider. The Chinese mobile market is developing along the same lines as Japan's DoCoMo's mobile market; both combine a cult of the cute with a passion for gadgetry. China's national culture has no diffusion drag because people are unwilling to adopt new technology. In this way, the Chinese are similar to the Japanese because neither the time nor the country effects of diffusion have much of an impact on the sale and use of mobile phones in East Asia.

In summary, some Chinese, Japanese, American, and European firms made good mobile phone investments in mainland China. They assessed cultural risk and did what was necessary to introduce value-added services in their mobile phones. The regional-local mobile phone strategies of these firms are a great success.

Microsoft provides exclusive new games in Japan's mature market

Japan's market for games, such as PlayStation 2 consoles, Sega's Dreamcast, and Nintendo GameCube machine, is mature. Sales for international celebrities of Pokémon, Sonic the Hedgehog, and Super Mario have peaked. Microsoft wants to break into this market with its Xbox console with games that Japanese customers have never seen before. Microsoft needs many new titles because it will make money on its software and not on its hardware. The question for Microsoft is as follows: Is Xbox the best technology that outdistances its competitors in Japan? If the answer is yes, then Xbox will be successful at least in the short term in Japan.

In summary, Microsoft faces an uphill battle in the Japanese games market. Domestic marketing is the most important theme in this contest over market share in the mature market for games in Japan. The local games strategy of both Japanese- and American-owned firms is difficult to accomplish given the total market is mature in Japan.

South East Asia confronts network effects

In August 2001, Japan was again flirting with a deep recession. Taiwan recorded GDP growth of 1.1 percent. The South Korea, Malaysian, and Hong Kong economies are decelerating sharply. Even Singapore has seen its economy go down slightly by 0.9 percent. The reason for these declines has been the collapse of spending on information technology equipment, the overall weakness of the US economy, and, of course, September 11, 2001. Electronic goods used to account for 55% of Singapore's exports to the USA; none are being shipped today. The same is true for laptops from Taiwan, many other consumer electronic products from the region, and auto parts from India, too.

In summary, South and South East Asia's consumer electronics and auto parts industries are going down fast throughout these regions. None of these countries has a large enough domestic market to take up the slack in demand. If the USA falls even further in the wake of the terrorist attack on September 11, 2001, then these countries and regions will bear the heavy burden of a deep recession throughout the developed world. Microeconomic data needs to be collected to show how fast these declines will be and what their long-term impact will be on national and regional markets.

Nation-states and regions must be smart movers

First-mover advantage has accrued to firms in northern Mexico, south-western England and northern Italy, and coastal Shanghai and southern Hong Kong, China. All of these regions have good brand name recognition. They are not timid about pushing their qualities as industrial clusters for both heavy and light industries. None of them want to be first followers.

Nevertheless, southern and southeastern Brazil, eastern Germany and Poland-A, Manchuria, and other regions prefer a wait-and-see attitude rather than trying to get out in front of the world development curve. They got their timing wrong because they did not know what race they were running against other regions. Most had a dead on arrival (DOA) feeling about them. None of these other regions of the world were smart movers.

Regions that are smart movers find business firms that are smart movers, too. These firms, such as Wal-Mart, Z.R.E., AIG, and Linktone, put together sound international business decisions, unlock profitable national cultures, and play on the strengths of heterogeneous agents among nations. None of these firms were slow learners. Instead, they were smart movers. In summary, all three elements of global strategy were at work in making these firms and the regions in which they were located successful in global-regional and national markets.

Prepare new models for the future

Global strategy puts together ideas from international business, country risk, and microeconomics and management strategy, then sorts them out in new ways, and helps business executives prepare for the future. For example, exports and imports or foreign trade was the dominant theme during the first era of globalization (1870–1914), through the Roaring Twenties, the Great Depression, and World War II. Then IB scholars looked at new foreign direct investment in postwar Europe and called it the American challenge. Later they studied European and Japanese investment in the USA. Over the course of two decades, foreign direct investment by US, European, and Japanese firms spread throughout the world. FDI supplanted foreign trade as the dominant theme of international business. Now IB scholars had to spend more time weighing the risks associated with countries, their economies, and national cultures, and the impact of country risk on sales growth and profitability overseas. Most recently, microeconomic data have become available to study firms as multicontract organizations and how they deal with or react to nation-states as heterogeneous agents in the world economy.

Let's re-sort all three ideas once again and see where we come out for the future:

International business

Today, American firms are outsourcing to Russian firms through partnerships, alliances, and nonequity joint ventures. (*Note*: foreign direct investments have taken a back seat to nonequity arrangements, as did foreign trade to FDI in a previous period.) Here is a short list of US-Russian deals:

» Vested Development, Inc. from Boston hires 200 Russian programmers in Moscow to tap out codes for US software firms.
» Intel has a software lab in Nizhny Novgorod.
» FastNet Solutions, Ltd in Moscow, an offshore programming company, is owned by an Irishman, but his Russian product is for US firms.
» Yukos, one of Russia's largest oil companies, commissioned Russian-owned information technology companies that have US partners to design and produce a computer-based human resources management system.
» Softlab in the Siberian city of Novosibirsk (at the Akademgorodok facilities) produces computer equipment that manipulates video images for use in television stations in partnership with Intel and Europe's Cern.
» Boeing operates a design center near the Kremlin in Moscow where Russian engineers modify a 777 for possible adoption into the fleet of Ilyushin and Tupolev planes.

Country risk

Today, European Russia and parts of Siberia are joining the west in a quest for links and stability among the market economies of Europe and the USA. Russia does not have a ruling Communist Party as is the case in China. Therefore, Russia can change its economic policy fast so long as its people and national culture are willing to adapt too. Engineers and scientists are willing to make these changes quickly, and they are being employed by the Russian partners or directly by American firms in Russia. For other Russians the time and country effects of diffusion will take awhile longer to overcome.

In 2001, Russia enjoyed strong growth. Its GDP rose by 5.1 percent through the second quarter of 2001. Industrial production also grew by 5.1 percent through August 2001. In the same period, the production of food and beverages expanded by 13.0 percent. Long-suffering Russian consumers in European Russia seem at last to be reaping much of the benefits.

Microeconomics and management strategy

Russian-American firms have both explicit and implicit contracts with Russian firms in Russia and with American firms in the USA. None of these deals are the same because the distribution of contracting rights among Russian-American firms varies widely based on when and under what circumstances old-world Russians became new-world Russian-Americans. Some are religious traditionalists or former Communists who are over 40 years old. These Old Russians lack up-to-date marketable skills. Others are entrepreneurs and market capitalists. They are under 40 years old. These New Russians have a monopoly on information technology and computer programming within Russia and in the Russian-American expatriate community in the USA.

US firms make side contracts with New Russian firms. Of course, transaction costs go up and profits decline because of the inefficiencies and unforeseen contingencies inherent in these nonequity arrangements. As a consequence, these New Russians have an opportunity for contractual opportunism, and they do change, update, and renegotiate their contracts with US firms. Right now, the New Russians in Russia together with their Russian-American counterparts in the USA have the opportunity to gain additional first-mover incentives over other firms seeking nonequity deals in Russia.

Old into New Russians

Here is a short list:

1 When Russia sold Alaska to the US in the 19th century, Russian nationals became American citizens. They spread from their rural peasant culture in Alaska and the West Coast to the urban centers of New York and Chicago. Until the Communist revolution of 1917, these Russians were loyal to their traditionalist Moscow church.

Then they had to make their own way into the wider enterprise and religious cultures of the USA. Today, only the most enterprising still speak Russian, but they are the ones who are doing the deals between Russia and the USA. Let's call them the St Vlad Russian-Americans.

2 After the Russian Communist revolution, white Russians (or the Czarists) fled Russia, settled first in the 17th *arrondissement* of Paris, then in Long Island, and later throughout northern New Jersey and New York state. Never loyal to the post-Communist Moscow church, these Russian-Americans became even more traditionalist with their own exile church. They too try to do deals between the two countries, but they lack the backing of Russia's president and the Moscow church. Let's call them the Jordanville Russian-Americans.

3 After the Chinese Communist revolution of 1948, some of the white Russians who had settled in Shanghai had to flee once again to San Francisco. Although some became St Vlad and others became Jordanville Russian-Americans, most learned mercantile skills in Shanghai and later became skillful deal makers between China and Russia, and the USA.

4 Then came the collapse of the Soviet Union in 1991 and a new flood of Russians to the USA. They were joined by Armenians, Russian Jews, and others. All saw an opportunity to make money in new careers in the USA. The Russian Orthodox among them joined the St Vlad Russian-American community.

Groups 1 and 4, together with some from group 3, are able to provide better and more complete information on Russia, and they are able to bring key Russian institutions (such as the president and the Moscow church) into partnerships with US firms. Group 2 presents many unforeseen contingencies. These Jordanville Russian-Americans raise up transaction costs for all who seek slimmed-down, nonequity deals between Russia and the USA.

Business deals

Some second and third generation Russian-Americans returned to Russia after 1991 to set up newspapers, magazines, TV stations, and advertising agencies. More stayed in the USA, joined forces with others from the former Soviet Union, and set up new businesses in the USA, such as Cybiko, a pocket organizer and wireless communicator for children. This firm does its research and development in Moscow, manufacturing in Taiwan, and its sales effort in Bloomingdale, Illinois.

Another Russian company known by the acronym IBS uses Adobe's PDF technology with an Internet connection and a printer to deliver local newspapers in all languages anywhere in the world. It is backed by the US venture capitalist, Esther Dyson. Their US firm is known as NewspaperDirect and it is responsible for selling the service to world travelers, business executives on the run, and others who want to keep in touch with home.

Both Cybiko and IBS (NewspaperDirect) are prototypes of future multicontract firms. They have a Russian past, a US present, and a Russian-US future. In 2001, electronics and communication devices for young people have carved a US $215 million niche in the US $22 billion-a-year toy industry. Cybiko toys are sold in Comp USA and F.A.O. Schwarz in the USA. On the other hand, IBS has yet to cover its costs of printing and delivery in hotel rooms. In the future, IBS will need more incentives to succeed while Cybiko will need fewer such incentives. No doubt the world economy will see more and different multicontract incentives as alliances, partnerships, and nonequity joint ventures become a staple of Russia's place in the west through strong ties to the EU and the USA.

With the ability to dig down deeply into micro socio-economic data, to look at the history of populations, and find out the rationale for crucial investment and partnership decisions, business executives can plan properly for the future. The Russian-American alliances, partnerships, and nonequity joint ventures are simply examples of what to expect in the future. The world economy is changing. Both nation-states and business firms must make crucial adjustments in their global strategy.

Keep reading about international business, country risk, and economics and management strategy. Keep sorting and re-sorting them over and over again. Make these ten steps your "To Do" list for the future.

SOURCES

Guy Chazan, "Now available from Russia: software programming," *The Wall Street Journal*, August 6, 2001, pp. B1-4

Michael R. Czinkota and Masaaki Kotabe, "Bypassing barriers to marketing in Japan," in Czinkota and Ilkka A. Ronkainen, eds., *Best Practices in International Business* (New York: Harcourt College Publishers, 2001): 299-309.

"Emerging-market indicators," *The Economist*, September 29, 2001, p. 102.

Peter S. Green, "A high-tech lifeline in Europe's rust belt," *The New York Times*, April 29, 2001, p. BU 5.

Gary Hamel, "Smart mover, dumb mover," *Fortune*, September 3, 2001, pp. 191-195.

Alexandra Harney, "Enter the dragon salesman," *Financial Times*, May 18, 2001, p. 12.

Jean-Jacques Laffont and David Martimort, "The firm as a multicontract organization," *Journal of Economics and Management Strategy*, 6:2 (Summer 1997): 201-234.

Joe Leahy and Richard McGregor, "Pets show the way for China's mobile services," *Financial Times*, August 30, 2001, p. 19.

Elizabeth Stanton, "An international toy with a Japanese accent," *The New York Times*, September 30, 2001, p. BU 6.

Sabrina Tavernise, "Boeing's Russian edge," *The New York Times*, May 26, 2001, pp. B1-2.

Sabrina Tavernise, "A technology delivers the dailies to some new doorsteps," *The New York Times*, October 1, 201, p. C15.

Astrid Wendlandt, "Russian hide and seek," *Financial Times*, March 27, 2001, p. 14.

Frequently Asked Questions (FAQs)

Chapter 1
» What is country risk?
» How does Wal-Mart pursue a global-regional strategy?
» Is Wal-Mart's strategy the same as McDonald's global strategy?
» What makes Wal-Mart a success in Canada and Mexico?
» Can Wal-Mart translate these successes outside the NAFTA countries?
» Why is an FTA strategy so important to the success of Wal-Mart in North America?

See the Wal-Mart case for the answers.

Chapter 2
» What is country risk?
» How do the European firms pursue a global-regional strategy?
» Are their strategies the same as those of McDonald's and Wal-Mart's global strategies?
» What makes MSN a success in Europe?
» Can European firms translate these successes outside the EU countries?

» Why is an FTA strategy so important to the success of these European firms in North America?

See Chapter 2 for the answers.

Chapter 3

» What is cultural risk?
» How do the Japanese auto firms pursue global-regional and domestic strategies?
» What makes Ford and Mazda a successful equity joint venture?
» What keeps Honda and Toyota independent?
» What makes Nissan-Renault a success in Japan, in North America, and in Europe?
» Can GM translate its Japanese alliances into a successful East Asian strategy?
» Why is an FTA strategy so important to the success of Japanese auto firms in North America and Europe?

See Chapter 3 for the answers.

Chapter 4

» What is country risk?
» How do Chinese joint ventures pursue regional and domestic strategies?
» Are intra-firm agreements and inter-firm contracts of equal importance, or is one set better than the other to grow sales?
» What are the realistic possibilities of switching the purchase of parts and components from intra-firm networks and their *keiretsu* to inter-firm market-based transactions?
» Will China's entry into the WTO expand its trade and investment opportunities?

See Chapter 4 for the answers.

Chapter 5

» How do nation-states (and their regions) create a brand image?
» What is brand capital? Experience goods?

» How do FTAs affect the value chain?
» What are value-based strategies?
» Of what importance are regions and their development strategy?

See Chapter 5 for the answers.

Chapter 6

» Why is global strategy important today? Why will global strategy be even more important tomorrow?
» How do neighboring countries, such as the USA and Canada or the USA and Mexico, differ from one another?
» Does cultural similarity bring about managerial carelessness?
» Do heterogeneously different countries alter the strategies of business firms?
» What does it take in the form of incentives to switch firms from one nation to another?
» Do emerging regions have to wait until their nations join FTAs to get the full benefit of the incentive they provide to foreign investors?

See Chapter 6 for the answers.

Chapter 7

» What modifications must be made in global strategy to take into consideration pre- and post-FTA heterogeneous behavior?
» How did Mexico's auto industry cluster jump ahead of Canada's auto industry cluster?
» Which type of knowledge is embedded into local subsidiaries?
» Why should parent firms make explicit contracts between themselves and their local subsidiaries?

See Chapter 7 for the answers.

Chapter 8

» What are the ten most important concepts in global strategy?
» Who are the most important thinkers in the field of international strategy?
» How do the concepts and thinkers shape the future of global strategy?

See Chapter 8 for the answers.

Chapter 9

» What do seminal articles tell practitioners on how to do a better job in global strategy?

» What new books and articles should practitioners and scholars be reading today?

See Chapter 9 for the answers.

Chapter 10

» Which global strategy steps come first, second, and third?

» Are all global strategy steps equally important?

» Which up-and-coming firms will join the list of multinational and multi-local firms?

» How do we know when potential Russian partners should joint the ranks of crucial international business strategists?

See Chapter 10 for the answers.

Index

Printed and bound by CPI Group (UK) Ltd, Croydon, CR0 4YY

13/04/2025

14656558-0005